Praise for
Forking Fantastic!

"This eccentrically enjoyable book by two strange and wonderful women may well be the cookbook America needs right now. Fun, deliberately unintimidating and filled with interesting—even ingenious—recipes, it inspires the nonprofessional to raise their game—and have a good time while doing so. Both book and authors are clearly good for the world."

—Anthony Bourdain

"We all know that something special happens when a bunch of people sit down together to share a meal, and for some reason there are too few family suppers happening. This book will help you relax, remind you to slug some wine for courage and inspire you to corral some friends and friendly strangers. Like the best hosts, their book is full of great stories and is generous with advice and encouragement. Cheers to more Sunday night suppers—on any day, at any hour!"

—Naomi Pomeroy, chef and cofounder of ripe Family Supper; chef/owner of Beast

"Ah yes—peek, and much more . . . into what these gals get excited about, and share in delicious bites. You too will discover your inner chef; I know I have."

—Michael Recchiuti, author of *Chocolate Obsession*

"In *Forking Fantastic!* Tamara and Zora share their gift of creating easy and delicious meals with wonderful stories, tips and recipes—reminding us all that good food is about sitting around a table and eating, drinking, talking, and laughing."

—Ana Sortun, chef/owner of Oleana Restaurant and author of *Spice*

Forking Fantastic!

PUT THE PARTY BACK IN DINNER PARTY

Zora O'Neill and Tamara Reynolds

GOTHAM BOOKS

GOTHAM BOOKS
Published by Penguin Group (USA) Inc.
375 Hudson Street, New York, New York 10014, U.S.A.
Penguin Group (Canada), 90 Eglinton Avenue East, Suite 700, Toronto, Ontario M4P 2Y3, Canada (a division of Pearson Penguin Canada Inc.) • Penguin Books Ltd, 80 Strand, London WC2R 0RL, England • Penguin Ireland, 25 St Stephen's Green, Dublin 2, Ireland (a division of Penguin Books Ltd) • Penguin Group (Australia), 250 Camberwell Road, Camberwell, Victoria 3124, Australia (a division of Pearson Australia Group Pty Ltd) • Penguin Books India Pvt Ltd, 11 Community Centre, Panchsheel Park, New Delhi—110 017, India • Penguin Group (NZ), 67 Apollo Drive, Rosedale, North Shore 0632, New Zealand (a division of Pearson New Zealand Ltd) • Penguin Books (South Africa) (Pty) Ltd, 24 Sturdee Avenue, Rosebank, Johannesburg 2196, South Africa

Penguin Books Ltd, Registered Offices: 80 Strand, London WC2R 0RL, England

Published by Gotham Books, a member of Penguin Group (USA) Inc.

First printing, October 2009
10 9 8 7 6 5 4 3 2 1

Photo credits: p. 1—Nicole Golden; p. 4—Zora O'Neill; p. 9—Elizabeth Bougerol; p. 10—Grant Jordan; pp. 17, 26—Karl Wasserman; p. 39—Peter C. Moskos; p. 40—Larra Nebel; pp. 61, 81, 93—Zora O'Neill; pp. 95, 99, 105—Karl Wasserman; p. 125—Zora O'Neill; p. 139—Jon Coifman; p. 151—Grant Jordan; pp. 187, 189, 203—Zora O'Neill; p. 205—Larra Nebel; p. 206—Peter C. Moskos, with illustration courtesy of Ali El Sayed; p. 223—Karl Wasserman. *Color insert*: p. 1, *top to bottom*—Karl Wasserman, Zora O'Neill, Peter C. Moskos; p. 2—Zora O'Neill (*3*); p. 3—Karl Wasserman (*3*); p. 4: Karl Wasserman (*top*), Zora O'Neill (*bottom*); p. 5—Karl Wasserman (*top and bottom*), Zora O'Neill (*middle*); p. 6—Karl Wasserman (*top*), Zora O'Neill (*2*); p. 7—Peter Moskos (*2*); p. 8—Grant Jordan (*top*), Karl Wasserman (*middle*), Zora O'Neill (*bottom*). *Cover*: Karl Wasserman. *Illustrations*: Christopher Calderhead.

Information on Spanish seamen's cuisine on page 8 reprinted by permission of LM Sorré. Biscuit recipe on page 176 reprinted by permission of Millicent Souris.

Gotham Books and the skyscraper logo are trademarks of Penguin Group (USA) Inc.

LIBRARY OF CONGRESS CATALOGING-IN-PUBLICATION DATA

O'Neill, Zora.
    Forking Fantastic!: Put the party back in dinner party / Zora O'Neill and Tamara Reynolds.—1st ed.
        p.   cm.
    ISBN 978-1-592-40505-3 (pbk.)
    1. Dinners and dining.   2. Entertaining.   I. Reynolds, Tamara.   II. Title.
TX737.O54 2009
641.5—dc22   2009010182

Printed in the United States of America
Set in Adobe Garamond
Designed by Elke Sigal

While the author has made every effort to provide accurate telephone numbers and Internet addresses at the time of publication, neither the publisher nor the author assumes any responsibility for errors, or for changes that occur after publication. Further, the publisher does not have any control over and does not assume any responsibility for author or third-party Web sites or their content.

TO PETER AND KARL

• CONTENTS •

CHAPTER 5

SUPER-SECRET CHAPTER FOR VEGETARIANS ONLY! · *67*

PART II

Four Foolproof Menus (Proofed by Us Fools) · *81*

SPRING LAMB · *85*

SUMMER IN THE YARD · *100*

FALL MEANS HAM · *108*

WINTER AND YOUR INNER BRAISE · 119

EAT YOUR VEGETABLES! · 130

FOR EXTRA CREDIT: LANE CAKE, DAPPER-STYLE · 133

PART III

Get In Over Your Head ·

FRIED CHICKEN FOR A CROWD · 143

LAST WORDS

Forking Fantastic!

INTRODUCTION

What kind of food do you cook? When people find out we run an underground supper club, that's often the first question out of their mouths.

We usually eyeball whoever's asking. If we're feeling polite, we say something vague about Southern and French (Tamara) or Middle Eastern and Indian (Zora). But the honest answer is simply: *fucking fantastic food.*

Election Day Café 2004: We survived with wine and coffee.

The ones who laugh when we say that, and nod in understanding—they'd fit right in with everyone who has been coming to our Sunday Night Dinners in Astoria, Queens, since 2003. They get that food doesn't have to be trendy, or authentic, or totally organic. They're happy to eat a Turkish street snack along with something we just happened to find in the market in our fabulously diverse neighborhood. They try out recipes from whatever cookbook we're reading, and from ex-mothers-in-law. They savor the best greens from the farmers' market,

1

but also anything that looks good at the corner grocer. All our guests—and we—care about is: Is it fucking fantastic?

Along with this basic principle, we're convinced that lounging around a big table after a multicourse feast, with the wine bottles nearly empty and the candles burning low, is one of the finer pleasures in life. All the work we've put into teaching ourselves to cook over the years culminates in this simple yet infinitely variable—and always satisfying—activity. Sunday Night Dinner began as a group of friends sitting around watching Sunday night TV. It has expanded into a twice-a-month supper club that's open to friends and friends-we-haven't-met-yet alike. Although we may cook dinner for twenty any day of the week, we still call it Sunday Night Dinner, because that's the spirit every event shares: a chance to sit together around a table, regroup, restore, debate and generally enjoy our free time.

THE SUNDAY NIGHT DINNER STORY

We met in 2002, after several years in New York with virtually no money. As an actress, Tamara opened off-off-Broadway plays, but had spent even more time as a server at new restaurants like Mario Batali's Babbo and Rocco DiSpirito's Union Pacific. Then she took a far less stuffy gig waiting tables at Prune. Zora was considering a career change from freelance writer to café proprietor and talked her way into a line-cook job at Prune, a restaurant whose chef-owner, Gabrielle Hamilton, she admired for both her food and her writing. At the Prune Christmas party, Zora overheard Tamara talking about grabbing a souvlaki in her neighborhood and correctly surmised that Tamara also lived in predominantly Greek Astoria, Queens. We promptly bonded over countless drinks, shared a cab home and woke up and couldn't remember any of the details of why we liked each other—just like a good first date.

No matter: We gradually pieced together that first conversation and very soon started cooking dinner together. Initially, the Sunday afternoon phone call from Tamara went something like this:

> "Hey, wanna come over and slow-cook a pork roast and some cranberry beans?"

Who says no to a suggestion like that? Zora hopped on her bike with a few ingredients from her corner greengrocer and invited her old college friend and new neighbor, Peter (fresh off a job as a police officer, finishing grad school and getting down with his Greek roots in Astoria), and his girlfriend, Amy. Tamara called her opera-singing pals, Victoria the Sicilian and the lovely Mary Ann, as well as Val, a fellow server at Prune and a Greek who also appreciated Astoria.

After a few months, that evolved into:

> "It's the *Sopranos* season premiere! Let's have a good old-fashioned red-checked-tablecloth dinner, with linguine with clams, bacalao fritters, Caesar salad and garlic bread!"

Hell, yes! By then, Tamara had had the pleasure of meeting Nicole (aka Golden), another neighbor, while doing a gay play involving lots of nudity and sacrilege—a bonding experience like no other. And Peter's friend Katie now lived nearby—and she could totally understand the logic of the casual dinner party, because she'd done the same thing when she lived up in Boston, except on Wednesdays. She brought her hot-pink pants and some tasty blueberry pies, along with Boston veteran Joel and his girlfriend, Deb.

Not too long after, things started to snowball. Tamara would call Zora in a panic:

> "Holy shit! Golden wants to bring her other friend too, so I have to go back to the butcher before he closes! Do you think I can drink my gin and tonic on my way there if I leave it in the Mason jar? The cops won't arrest me or anything, will they? Ask Peter. And can you pick up some extra shallots on your way over?"

We rose to the occasion every weekend, no matter who showed up. It's not like we set out to do anything big. We just started cooking together on Sunday nights because Tamara had a TV and there was good programming on, and everyone had to eat. When Tamara got TiVo, we no longer had to hustle to sit down in front of the TV—though we still tried to get an early start for the sake of regulars like Zora's college friend Karine, a high school teacher with brutally early mornings. We started to spend the whole day on ridiculous projects—such as when Tamara's friend Heather (better known as Mr. Shit) brought over some vintage Southern layer cake recipes. No watching TV meant Nicole could get the after-dinner dance party going in the kitchen, to entertain whoever was washing dishes. Now and then Tamara would invite a date.

Guests drop money in the donation box.

Looking back, the real turning point was when Tamara invited Dapper Dan (his parents named him Michael Johnson). He was a regular at Prune who was far too well dressed for his surroundings, and he earned Tamara's respect by eating everything in sight, often with his fingers. And even though she didn't know him too well, and didn't want to date him, she figured he was just the kind of person who'd enjoy our little Sunday gatherings.

He did. And he started inviting some of his friends. We went out and bought a few more folding chairs. And we carried on, spending the week scheming, planning bigger and more elaborate projects for ourselves. It was gratifying to read some intriguing recipe on Wednesday, then serve it to friends—and a few strangers—on Sunday. Zora had started writing travel guides, so she'd often come back with great ideas for dinner based on the tacos she'd eaten in Puerto Morelos or the greens she'd tasted in Aleppo. Tamara was still working as a waitress, so she got lots of ideas from fancy New York City chefs and her new Edna Lewis cookbook, a gift from Mr. Shit.

But then we noticed that we were both broke at the end of the month. Sunday Night Dinner was obviously the culprit. We tentatively asked for a donation—twenty bucks, maybe, if you've got it? Zora, who'd run a supper club before she met Tamara, knew they'd be lucky to break even, and didn't want to earn money off the project, lest it start feeling like a pain-in-the-ass job. But at least this step kept us from resenting all our hungry friends when it came time to write the rent check.

As it turned out, not only were people happy to donate, but this meant they could now invite their friends with impunity because it no longer cost anyone but the diner any money. The last-minute repeat runs to the butcher increased, and, as if the New York City government were smiling down on us, the liquor laws were relaxed, so guests could buy booze on Sundays, on the way over—thus the ". . . and a bottle of wine" phrase got added to the suggested donation. Sunday Night Dinner was officially born—although by that time we were having the party on Saturdays just as often.

Now we have an e-mail list of more than four hundred names and regularly cook for twenty people every couple of weeks. It's still not a job for either of us, and it's a surprise and a challenge every time we do it.

It's a surprise for everyone who comes as well—we rarely cook the same thing twice, nor is the guest list ever duplicated. It all starts with an e-mail invitation describing what we've decided to cook—sort of an extended explanation of "fucking fantastic food!"

How We Came to Kick Kitchen Ass

We cannot stress it enough: *We taught ourselves how to cook.* Which means you can too. And we went about it in different ways—which means whatever path you take will be the right one. Here's how we got where we are today:

ZORA	TAMARA
Raised in New Mexico. Mom had copy of *Larousse Gastronomique* but family often lived on food stamps. Important lessons about thrift, rare steak and nastiness of cheap chocolate imprinted at young age.	Raised in Arizona. Dad was a chef, until he quit drinking. Mom rolled out a mean strudel. Aspired not to cook, but "to be famous, and have other people cook for me!"
During grad school, finally forced to cook for herself. Cracked open copy of Indian cookbook from ex-boyfriend, subscribed to *Cook's Illustrated* and started experimenting on equally broke roommates.	During college, got married to a man who cooked. Sick of washing dishes every night, she thought, "How hard can it fucking be?" Subscribed to *Gourmet* and started experimenting on husband's Navy buddies.
Quit grad school. Moved to NYC without enough money.	Got divorced. Quit grad school. Moved to NYC without enough money.
Continued to cook, even though New Yorker friends considered her weird. Embraced world cuisines (i.e., beans and rice) because of severe underemployment.	Continued to cook, even though New Yorker friends considered her weird. Worked front of house for fancy restaurants, picking up recipes along the way.

We owe home cooking for getting us through some really rough financial spots. Tamara still often improvises something tasty she once ate in a restaurant, while Zora goes for a more researched style of homey dishes. Either way, we're constantly trying new things—and consistently pleased with how this one skill has changed our lives.

To: Sunday Night Dinner

Subject: Sunday Dinner This Sat., Oct. 14 @ 7 P.M.—Spain, Take 2!

Hey Hungry Kiddies—

I hope this finds you well and STARVING. Due to the holiday weekend, we decided to postpone the celebration of Cristóbal Colón and his bankroller, Spain, to THIS Saturday, Oct. 14 @ 7 P.M. Please RSVP by Friday, Oct. 13 @ 10 A.M., so I can Greenmarket accordingly.

What better thing to eat this post–Columbus Day weekend than some Spanish food? I know it is a tossup as to whether we should celebrate Italy or Spain, but we thought we would put ourselves in Queen Isabella's shoes for this revisionist dinner. You may be given your own knife upon entrance, just like Columbus's sailors! Don't worry, though—no guest will be conquered or enslaved without their specific consent. If you are sitting on the fence for this one, scroll down and read what his sailors had to eat, and maybe you'll be swayed in our direction, if only out of thankfulness that you are here now and not then.

Oh—and the menu is as follows:

Spanish cured ham (that you will get your own knife to cut to your heart's desire!)

Catalan tomato bread

Boquerones

Maybe a saffron-and-potato tortilla?

Mackerel in escabeche

Watercress salad

Potato salad with mussels

Lentils with leeks and mushrooms

Forking Fantastic!

Orange-flower thingies (fried pâte à choux with orange-flower water)

Lemon fritters (oh wait—rereading recipe—it's lemon leaves OR
bay leaves, and you dip them in batter and fry, then eat them by
scraping the dough off the leaf with your teeth)

As for the booze, bring however much you think you will drink.
If, like us and some people we know, you are what some would
term a harmless drunk, then feel free to bring two bottles. We do.

Saturday Oct. 14, 2006 @ 7 P.M.
Reynolds/Wasserman/Trainor Ranch
Front deck or backyard, uncertain at this time

In love and garlic,
Tamara and Zora

---

* *According to LM Sorré, the menu for Spanish seamen consisted of water,
vinegar, wine, olive oil, molasses, cheese, honey, raisins, rice, garlic, almonds, sea
biscuits (hardtack), dry legumes such as chickpeas, lentils, beans, salted and
barreled sardines, anchovies, dry salt cod and pickled or salted meats (beef and
pork) and salted flour. The olive oil and perhaps olives were stored in earthenware
jugs. All other provisions were stored in wooden casks, which, according to some
reports, were of cheap and faulty construction, permitting the preserving brine
to leak out of the meat casks and allowing moisture to invade the casks of dry
provisions. All were stored in the hold, the driest section of which was normally
reserved for casks carrying dry provisions. A cooper (barrel maker) was
responsible for keeping the casks tight, an almost impossible challenge.*

*Food, mostly boiled, was served in a large communal wooden bowl. It
consisted of poorly cooked meat with bones in it, the sailors attacking it with
fervor, picking it with their fingers as they had no forks or spoons. The larger
pieces of meat were cut with the knife each sailor carried.*

From there, the RSVPs roll in fast and furious—all twenty seats are usually taken within the day. Come the weekend, these brave people arrive at the door, clutching their bottles of wine. Some come in groups—regular guests bringing new friends—and some come alone. Some have heard about us through the grapevine, and others are people we've met and wanted to get to know better—so we invited them to dinner. For many guests, it's their first time coming to Queens (New York's most unfashionable borough, we're a little proud to say).

People are always boggled that we let total strangers into our home. We're more impressed that total strangers are willing to *come* to our home. For all they know, we could be axe murderers or white slavers. We at least know they like to eat, because they answered the e-mail. It only adds to their nervousness when neither of us answers the door—we're too busy cooking. Usually it's Tamara's husband, Karl, who lets people in, hands them a jelly jar for their wine and shows them around. New guests seem pretty relieved by the time they make it to the kitchen—we look normal enough, even if we're sweaty, wild-eyed and flinging cast-iron skillets around.

All of what would be the counter space is covered with food in various states of preparation. Led Zeppelin is blaring, spices are scattered all over the place and the room smells unbelievably good—savory, garlicky, rich. But no sooner do these people take in the scene and introduce themselves to us than we have to stop everything and shoo them back to the living room. Tamara's not

We ask guests to bring as much wine as they expect to drink . . .

...**and we do our best to drink it all.**

one to mince words: "Hey, so glad you could come—now we need you all to get the fuck out of the kitchen so we can finish your dinner!" The music gets cranked louder, and people go running. We can't actually say what happens at the parties for the next hour or so—but people tell us it usually involves heated discussions about politics, religion, street food in Vietnam and the relevance of 1970s thrillers. By the time we emerge with dinner completed, everyone seems to be fast friends.

We serve everything family-style, around a couple of tables set with mismatched plates, dishcloths for napkins and odd pieces of silver-plate cutlery. Wine flows liberally, and by the time the night has wound down, the bottles are empty and the candles spent. Sometimes we have to kick the last few stragglers out, but not before they make sure they're on the guest list for good.

What's so special about Sunday Night Dinner—what our regulars keep coming back for, because they can't get it anywhere else—is that it's just like a regular family dinner at home (without gropey Uncle Fester). In short, we're not pretending to be a restaurant. We're not into matchy-matchy shit and pretty garnishes and cookbooks from the latest hot chef—all that is just trying to imitate the dining-out experience. The great thing about eating at home is we're *at home*. We can lounge around as long as we like—or until the neighbors complain about the raucous late-night bullshitting. No one's going to drop the check and make us feel like we should clear out for the next customers. If people want seconds or thirds, they can help themselves. If they overhear a good conversation to their left, they can jump in. If they want a recipe, all they have to do is ask and we'll write it down on a scrap of butcher paper. We've cooked Sunday Night Dinner in a number of different apartments along the way. Each place has been imperfect (small, dusty, still furnished with late-postcollege starter pieces) but each has hosted perfect meals—because it's home.

WHY SUNDAY NIGHT DINNER?

So, do you make money off this? is the second most common question we get from people.

Hard to believe, but—no. We lavishly pay the dishwasher (sometimes an out-of-work friend, sometimes the busser from our favorite neighborhood diner), and the rest goes to keep the house stocked with good olive oil, kosher salt, spices and emergency wine for when dinners go especially late. We've gradually picked up additional chairs and dishes, so people no longer have to sit on cinder blocks or bring their own soup bowls. Before you know it, the cash is gone.

So why do you do it, then? That's the obvious follow-up question.

We do it because at every meal, our extended social community reknits itself in a fascinating way: The former priest turned calligraphy professor sits next to the design-school student; the hedge fund guy chats with the environmental activist. Neighbors drop by and meet people who live on the other side of the city. Sometimes they've all been crammed on a sofa together; sometimes they get to sprawl out in the yard and spot lightning bugs in the grass. But our "hungry kiddies" (as we've come to call them in our e-mail invitations) always surprise us with their willingness to eat just about anything we throw at them and their enthusiasm for talking to whoever winds up sitting in the next chair.

We know from experience: Some of the best friendships are forged around the dinner table—and in the kitchen. Together, we've had wild successes and a couple of sketchy failures. We've had parties for birthdays and the Fourth of July, and for no other reason than there were delicious figs at the produce stand. We had parties when we wanted to celebrate, and when we wanted to stay home and drink alone after a bad breakup. Through the course of five years of dinners, we both went from single to hitched to fantastic men. Tamara finally brought a date to dinner who clicked with the group—Karl now mans the grill, whips up ice cream and strips meat from carcasses like nobody's business. And Zora finally realized she loved her friend Peter—who has helped pave the way with Greek landlords and build spits and tables when called for. Over five years, Zora survived open-heart surgery (not due to her high-fat diet—don't worry!), and Tamara had to move three times and change jobs many more times. Good friends left the city, and new ones moved in. Throughout, the dinners have been our ritual and our creative outlet—it was doubly fortunate that our ever-expanding circle of friends got fed and happy in the bargain.

Oh, we feel the sentimental tears and the chick-flick soundtrack coming on. So let's talk about *you*.

WHY YOU SHOULD COOK DINNER

We're not saying you need to run out and start your own underground supper club. We actually wouldn't wish that on anyone. But we do want you to cook a little dinner for your friends, and maybe some of their friends, because we think it's a fucking shame that no one does this anymore. We're not making any promises, but once you get the nerve to serve, maybe you'll fall in love, start a new career or change your life some other way.

We realize there are some hurdles to overcome before this dinner party utopia is reached. The largest is simply cultural. For some reason, a candlelit, wine-sodden dinner is socially acceptable only in your bohemian midtwenties. And some people don't even get this postcollege slacker interlude—they graduate straight to takeout. After that, we're all supposed to be too busy with important things and too in love with our fancy grown-up furniture to risk spilling wine on it. But this is no different from our grandparents and their "good" furniture covered in plastic—a tragic waste. So keep the Tide stain stick at the ready, and invite your friends over.

And the success of Sunday Night Dinner is proof that you don't need a lot of gear to entertain your friends. Even if you didn't get china for your wedding, or you lost it in the divorce, or you just plain forgot to get married, you can still have

We Don't Have Kids . . .

. . . but we support those who do. We recognize it's a colossal amount of work, and if you have a little one or two, you're probably reading this book and saying, "As if!" But please don't give up. Cooking good dinners and eating them with friends and family is one of the most rewarding things kids can experience. At least we think so, because that's how we were raised. Modern American convenience food culture presses parents to "spend less time in the kitchen, and more time with your family!" Better: Spend time with your family *in the kitchen.* Exploit your child labor force—cooking with kids keeps them occupied, makes them feel useful and teaches them valuable life skills. Drafting your husband or wife to be the sous-chef can teach you a thing or two about teamwork and giving orders. And if your friends can't get sitters for the night of your big party, have them bring the kids. Let them hang out on the staircase in their jammies, like in a Rockwell painting. They'll watch the adults and learn . . . and they'll be better for it in the long run.

a fucking fantastic dinner party. You don't need a mandoline (you don't even need to know what one is), you don't need a FryDaddy, you don't need matching flatware, you don't need any of the crap you see in magazines and on TV. Please ignore the trappings of obsessive perfectionism that surround the dinner party today: centerpieces, place cards, dainty food, polite conversation. All of these superficial things have nearly driven dinner parties to the brink of extinction.

What you *do* need are a few friends. If you're at all overscheduled like we are, even that element of the party can sometimes be difficult to muster. People are overworked and stressed out. They have kids and can't get a sitter. Press on: If your guests can't make a big-deal Saturday night, schedule a Sunday lunch or a simpler weeknight dinner. Even the most basic meal with friends can have amazing restorative powers. If someone's on the fence, remind them, as we often do to each other: "You gotta eat. And you may as well eat with friends." Even if you start out with only a couple of people, you'll wind up with more, once word gets out that you're known for cooking dinner.

We want you to succeed and have just as much fun in the kitchen as we've had. This book provides you with the courage you need to entertain for the sake of food and community, not for the prize of being the most brainwashed host(ess) on the block. To conquer the Dinner Party Wasteland, you just have to do your part and invite a few friends over to dinner. Set up your kitchen with help from our Cautious Beginners section, if you like, and start with the simple roast chicken dinner there. If you already feel even a little bit comfortable in the kitchen, then you can tackle anything in our Four Foolproof Menus section—all good weekend meals, pretested at our Sunday Night Dinners. And if you, like us, crave a challenge, then Get In Over Your Head, the final section of truly over-the-top special-occasion dinners, will get your brain kicked into high gear. And no need to begin at the front and work your way methodically through—the last menu, for roast lamb on a spit, is one of the first big meals we ever cooked together. In testing recipes for this book, we've consistently been amazed at how a challenge turns into a breeze on the second try—and we hope we've streamlined the process enough to help you through the first time.

Along the way, we've also included tips on shopping, organization and all-around attitude. And for anyone who doesn't know much about wine except that they like to drink it, we've included general suggestions for vino and other boozy treats throughout. These notes come from our many years of enthusiastically drinking wine and Tamara's many years of selling and serving it. If there's one lesson we've learned, it's this: Excellent, very drinkable wine can also be cheap. Most of the wines we suggest can be had for $15 per bottle, and some for $10 or less. (They're a guide only if you want it—it's more important that you just drink what you want to.)

But perhaps most useful are the boxes labeled LEARN FROM OUR MISTAKES! We hope you'll find some fabulous wisdom in them that saves you from failure—though you may just laugh your ass off at how we could be so stupid. We also understand that not everyone has the cash, time and Californian produce to be Alice Waters. We dig local, seasonal and organic, but we live in the real world. We understand the occasional off-season weakness, think canned black beans taste just fine and know there's nothing handier than a bag of frozen peas. With a few exceptions, the recipes use ingredients you can get in any large American supermarket. If

Terms & Conditions

In this book, we've used some rather vague terms of measurement—*glug,* for instance, when it comes to olive oil; *handful* when referring to herbs. We thank Jamie Oliver for first introducing these words to the cookbook lexicon, and we encourage you to get comfortable with them.

Whenever you see some imprecise measurement like this, don't stress out: The underlying message is that *the precise amount just doesn't matter that much.* We're sick and tired of recipes that command you to measure out "1½ tablespoons olive oil" (which is probably what a *glug* amounts to). Doing this takes a ridiculous amount of time, and it also means you have to wash those measuring spoons. The sooner you can shake off the tyranny of precise measurements, the faster you'll get to real cooking and learning to trust your instincts. (Baking, alas, is another story—there you do often have to measure things precisely. Which is probably why we don't do it that often.)

your area just doesn't have the ethnic diversity New York does, you may have to mail-order a couple of items (see Where to Get the Goods on page 228 for suggestions), but they're the kind of thing that will last you a good long time.

To be honest, we wrote this cookbook not only to help you but also to help *us.* That's because between the two of us, we've received only five invitations to dinner at other people's homes in the past year. (We do cuss a lot, but honestly, we're still great guests.) And we're getting a little tired of holding up our end. Our vision is this: We persuade you to get into the kitchen and cook, and then maybe you'll persuade your friends, and they'll persuade theirs, and pretty soon you'll all be inviting *us* to dinner.

But don't sit back and read for too long. Cooking dinner for your friends is one arena in which the glow of accomplishment can be gained in just a few hours. And it is a supremely generous gift that we believe beats the hell out of anything you can buy. Your friends are dying to be invited over, so damn it, give them a call. Take a chance, crank up the flames on your stove and cook some dinner! It just may be the best gift you give yourself (and maybe us?) all year.

Date: Monday, April 10, 2006
To: Sunday Night Dinner
Subject: Sunday Night Dinner . . . the Lord Has Risen Indeed! Easter 2006

Hey Hungry Kiddies—

Assuming I survive Passover, I would like to cordially invite you to an Easter Feast at the Hooray Christ Is Risen Headquarters, otherwise known as the Reynolds/Wasserman/Trainor Ranch. This will be the maiden Sunday Night Dinner voyage of our new living arrangement, so if the weather is nice, we could even eat outside in the backyard!!!!

On the menu is a Heritage Foods USA Red Wattle pork shoulder roast, some of the most amazing pork I have ever had the pleasure of tasting (heritagefoodsusa.com).

There will be as many spring veggies as I can get my little hands on (ramps!! ramps!!) and maybe even that fabulous Easter tradition, scalloped potatoes!! Please RSVP by Friday at 12 P.M. I am picking up the little Red Wattle roast that afternoon, and I want to be certain I get enough for all those who wish to partake.

Let's do a late afternoon/early supper. Arrive for garden cocktails at 4 P.M., dinner at 5.

Tamara Reynolds
Astoria, NY

PART I

Cautious Beginners, Start Here

Summer 2008:
Good food and booze bring
Tamara and Ian closer.

CHAPTER 1

THE PEP TALK

Starting to cook is sort of like starting to go to the gym. You can always do it tomorrow. In fact, we're *still* planning on tomorrow for the gym. But we did commit to learning to cook, and we're much happier—and healthier—for it, so we don't really need the damn gym anyway. Remember, we taught ourselves to do this—which means anyone can.

We see you, still sitting there all listless, thinking ahead to the Chinese takeout you're going to order for dinner. No! Listen up:

WHY YOU SHOULD LEARN TO COOK IF YOU HAVEN'T ALREADY . . .

1. Sex!

Cooking is like sex, in that at first it can seem a little messy and not worth all the trouble. Trust us, it gets *a lot* better. Similarly, food TV and chef worship is just like porn: Watching other people cook can be exciting, but it is nowhere near as satisfying as doing the deed yourself. And if you get too wrapped up in Giada De Laurentiis's fantasy world, you're going to feel too insecure to grab hold of your own whisk and [insert your own double entendre here].

People put an amazing amount of energy into getting laid, but you can get quite a lot of satisfaction from food as well—and you don't need to get dressed up and go out for happy hour to do it. In fact, we might go so far as to say cooking is better, or at least more reliable, than sex—and we can say this from plenty of experience in both fields.

Forking Fantastic!

SEX	COOKING
After the initial thrill wears off, you're looking at once a day, tops.	At least three times a day
Typically requires partner; partnerless can be rewarding, but only for so long.	You can do it all by yourself, and you don't have to share (but then it's nice too if you do).
After the initial thrill wears off, three or four standard positions	Endless variety
After the initial thrill, lasts ten or fifteen minutes	A quick dinner takes half an hour, and enjoying the meal takes another half an hour at least.
Can do it with friends, but it's hard to maintain	Can do it with friends—and it's even better
Economically risky: cost of one date, and who knows how many more before you get laid?	Economically sound: purchase food, add spice and fire and eat.
May require a booty call	Just look in your fridge.

And, practically speaking, cooking can get you through a long dry spell with a lot more self-respect. Sitting at home alone eating Domino's in front of sitcom reruns: sad. Sitting at home eating a mushroom omelet and a Bibb lettuce salad and washing it down with a glass of wine: sexy. And if you invite someone over to eat an omelet with you—well, then you'll have real friends and won't just have to watch them on TV.

We don't have the data to back this up, but we're pretty damn sure that people who know how to cook have a lot more sex. A standard date takes place in a restaurant. After all the hemming and hawing over the menu, the deliberating over how much to spend on wine without looking like an ass, the etiquette of sharing bites off each other's plates, you're still sitting there and no closer to either person's bed. So many dates that are on the edge limp to a halt when the reality of getting to one party's house together sets in.

But if you invite someone over for dinner, you're already that much closer to the bedroom—and then the deal is sealed when you serve up some seduction dish like roast duck for both of you. Plus, at home, you can lick your fingers—an incredibly sexy move—and no one will look at you funny.

2. Art!

Cooking is creative. Is your house crammed with half-finished knitting projects and wonky self-built bookcases that you never got around to putting the trim on? Switch to cooking as your creative outlet, and you'll get the gratification of finishing a project inside an hour—and you won't have to worry about where to store your finished project, because you will have eaten it all up and said, "Damn, I'm a genius!" When you're in the zone in the kitchen, your brain gets into that same relaxed yet focused Zen state as when you're pasting funny pictures around the border of your holiday letter, rearranging the furniture or drafting a really good complaint e-mail.

And if you think you're not a creative person and wonder why artists get to have all the fun, give cooking a try. It's a small art to compose a meal that's a good balance of flavors, colors and nutrients. It's also an art to pull a meal out of a seemingly empty fridge. But it's also a totally accessible art that doesn't require an M.F.A., grandiose statements or schmoozing with the nouveau riche.

3. Power!

When you cook your own food, you get to control exactly what you eat. We're obviously not diet freaks, but control is good. Why does the food at your favorite restaurant taste so savory? We hate to break it to you, but the answer is pretty much always the same: obscene amounts of fat (and often not even a normal, unprocessed fat like butter). Cook that same dish at home, rein in the butter a bit, add a fresh salad on the side with just the amount of dressing you want, and you're already better off than if you'd trundled down to the local branch of America's Best Restaurant in a Mall Parking Lot.

Scale down the portion from bigger-than-your-head to just normal, and you're a glowing picture of health. Skip the breadsticks, the pink cocktail and the two pounds of Rocky Road Gut-Buster Mocha Death for dessert (yeah, no—it doesn't really help if you share it), and you're totally crushing cheap-restaurant-food-induced gluttony with your newfound strength.

And of course you've been reading all about hydrogenated fats (shudder), factory-farm animals (OMG—they clip the beaks off chickens?!) and genetically modified vegetables (jury's out on actual danger, but still creepy). Restaurants are so far not required to disclose where all their food comes from and just how full of pesticides it is, but until then, you can pretty safely assume that all but the most splurgeworthy or super-righteous joints are just getting what's cheapest from their purveyors, and that means beakless, pesticide-laden nastiness.

But wait—we're *not* saying your home kitchen should be totally organic and free-range and virtuous in every way. Start however you can—with a can of refried beans, if you have to. Spend whatever you feel comfortable spending. Zora's path from off-label "bacon misshapes" during grad school to half a joyously happy heritage-breed pig took more than a decade and a move into a higher tax bracket. That's why, in this cookbook, we certainly encourage you to buy good ingredients, but our recipes will not call for, say, "1 lovingly caressed, clear-eyed, certified clean Sicilian Buttercup hen—and if you can't get that, give up now." Getting back to the concept of control, when you buy your own ingredients, you know what they are and (at least a little) where they came from.

4. Stickin' It to The Man!

Oh, you're a feminist, and you didn't work this hard to spend your life in the kitchen? That's good, sister. But see above re: control. Power is yours for the taking in the kitchen, both when you're deciding what to eat and when you're feeding other people. When you cook a meal for someone, you're not lying down on the linoleum and asking the patriarchy to trample you. You're telling someone you love them and care about their pleasure and their health. Ain't nothin' sexist about that. Sexy, maybe—but not sexist.

Moreover, you may have noticed how the world of high-powered cheffery just oozes testosterone: military-style chain of command, public shouting matches and competitive meat consumption. A wise friend of ours opined that this was due to men having to overcompensate for doing what's perceived as "women's work." Likely true, but the macho chef dudes are on to something: It *is* fun to wield big, sharp knives and swear like a sailor, even if it's totally unnecessary for making food that tastes good. Try it—we think you'll like it.

. . . AND WHY YOU SHOULDN'T WORRY TOO MUCH ABOUT BEING A GOOD COOK

Brilliant, you're saying—but I can't even make a damn omelet! Does toast count as dinner?

Yes, it does, if you put cheese on top of it and eat some greens on the side. Start slow. Just as you don't have to be buying aspirational chickens and fruit worth its weight in gold, you don't need to be cooking five-course extravaganzas straight out of the gate, and no one expects you to.

The point of this book—and of all home cooking, really—is to have your friends and family over for dinner, and have a nice time while sitting around the table. You don't want to plop down a big bag of Mickey D's in front of everyone, like a ton of despair. But even if you're a kitchen delinquent, it's completely acceptable to open up a bag of lettuce, boil up some pasta and pour prefab sauce over it (tip: crumble in some bacon, or stir in some gorgonzola). It will taste just fine.

Your first attempts at cooking will probably yield some flops—but that's fine too. All that motivational crap about learning from your mistakes is actually true when it comes to cooking—unlike in, say, relationships. You may not be able to give up dating drummers, but if you spatter tomato sauce all over your cabinets once, you'll be sure to turn the heat down and put a lid on it the next time.

As much as we talk about it for the whole rest of this book, the food is not the point, really. The food is just the means to nourishing yourself and the people you love best.

A Note on Health

Looking through this book and seeing all the duck fat involved, you probably won't believe us when we say that we care about being healthy. No, really, we do. We care in an old-fashioned way. Like:

- Eat your vegetables. More greens never hurt.
- Don't count calories—just eat less junk. You know you can't make up for a 1,200-calorie mochaccino just by munching celery the rest of the day.
- Drink wine. It keeps your blood thin. But don't mention the words *antioxidant* and *polyphenol.* Just drink the wine.
- Laugh your ass off. Pun intended.
- Food is good for you. Don't be afraid of it.

And that's all we're going to say about *that*.

CHAPTER 2

ANATOMY OF A DINNER PARTY

"**D**inner party"—it just sounds so, ew, *formal,* right? So grown-up, so seating-arranged, so wife-swapping after the liqueurs.

In fact, dinner parties can take many, many forms. The essential elements—food and people to eat it—don't change, but just about everything else can be tweaked to fit how you live.

Start by ignoring all existing mainstream advice on the subject. It's easy to chortle at the hyperperfectionist discussions of chilled butter balls and salad forks imparted in, say, Tamara's vintage edition of *How to Give Successful Dinner Parties,* a book in the Amy Vanderbilt Success Program for Women series—ah, 1963, so ridiculous! But then we nearly choke with outrage when we flip open the latest issue of *Martha Stewart Living* and see a how-to for some winsome handcrafted centerpiece for your harvest-theme dinner for eight.

It's not that we think La Stewart is a vision of retro horror who's keeping women in chains—it's just that centerpieces are totally impractical. Quite simply, if you build some elaborate thing out of hand-foraged deer antlers and fair-trade sequins, uh, *where will you put the damn food?*

Throwing a dinner party is not an exercise in creating a tabletop wonderland, nor is it about imitating the formality and frills of a restaurant. It's about sitting around a table and eating, drinking and talking. One of the best dinner parties Zora ever attended involved the hostess serving house-brand canned tomato soup and later getting so drunk she fell down in the kitchen. Over eight hours, the candles melted away, the red wine got drained and the guests solved all the world's problems through hearty debate. Zora does try to avoid canned soup and falling down drunk but still holds this party up as a parable for what success can be gained

Forking Fantastic!

The best centerpiece of all: food and wine

when you just say, "Fuck it," and stick to the basics.

So put down the persimmon place mats and the twig-shaped place card holders, and focus your creative energies on inviting friends, making shopping lists and perhaps even cooking. The best "tablescape" has food in the middle of it and your friends seated around the edges. Here's all you need to know for dinner party success, in handy FAQ format.

Dinner Party FAQs

1. How many people do I invite?
2. What do I cook?
3. I thought you said food wasn't so important, really. Can't I just get some nice takeout?
4. I can't do this alone!
5. Help! I don't have any furniture! Or silverware! Or . . . ! Or . . . !
6. Help! I don't have any friends!
7. What else am I forgetting?

1. HOW MANY PEOPLE DO I INVITE?

There are generally two routes a dinner party can take in terms of guests. The safe and reasonable path is to keep the total number of attendees at ten or fewer. This will prevent you from hyperventilating from stress, and it will also keep the guest interaction a little more controlled. Each end of the table can break into separate conversations, but if someone has a really good story to tell, she can tell it without feeling like she's peering at a packed house over the vaudeville footlights.

Anything more than ten but less than about sixteen people can be a little awkward. Chances are slim you have a single table that can seat everyone, and even so, there are going to be some people who feel stuck between larger conversations, turning this way and that, trying to keep up with a bad-date story on one side and a political debate on the other. So if you're not keeping it small, then go big. Our dinners are typically twenty people, which sounds like a lot, but it's a reasonable number when spread over two tables. Twenty people is also enough to make the early evening feel more like a chatty cocktail party. This is fantastic if you're still in the kitchen freaking out over all the stuff you have left to cook—the guests can entertain each other, and probably won't even notice you back there cursing and wailing. And once you've cooked dinner for twenty, dinner for eight is a cakewalk.

2. WHAT DO I COOK?

We'll get to that in a lot more detail later, but first and foremost, please ignore that dull advice, repeated in every guide to entertaining, about always using recipes you've cooked before. Think about the last time you busted a move in the sack—had you practiced that before you brought it out for a stranger? Probably not. Likewise, if you have a hankering for a leg of lamb, go for it. When the hell else are you going to make it, except for a group of friends? The list of things we've cooked for the first time in front of a crowd is long and terrifying: fried chicken, cassoulet, paella on a grill, whole roast lamb on a spit. . . . But as long as you're moderately organized and can block out the panicked voice in your head, you'll be fine cooking anything for the first time. Booze works, of course, but so does this mantra: "There's always pizza." Breathe deep, and repeat it as necessary. Remember, if it weren't for you, your friends would probably be home shaking a frozen veggie burger out of the box—so they're already better off.

Also, although we admire the standard advice about choosing dishes that can all be prepared beforehand, we never really stick to it. Wouldn't it be lovely if, when our guests arrived at the door, we were standing around, all freshened up in a pretty little apron and holding a cold drink, ready to greet everyone warmly and personally? Yes, it might seem nicer than running out of the shower barely covered by the hand towel you had in there, dripping wet and blathering like a maniac. But it would be totally dull. Zora did manage to pull everything together early once, and without all the activity in the kitchen, everyone just sat around awkwardly in the living room for a forced chitchat period, thinking, *So why aren't we eating already?*

We probably have a secret addiction to chaos, but we also get derailed by special festive-occasion dishes that just beg to be added to the menu. Things that require deep-frying are especially tempting—we can't resist the alchemy that occurs in oil at 350°F, even though we know this magic has to happen at exactly the last minute before serving. Like drinking alone, deep-frying alone is a sign of trouble, and we don't condone it. Friends, however, provide the perfect excuse for making squash blossom fritters or perfecting your french fries. But if you do tackle something elaborate, round it out with easier things. One difficult dish per dinner is enough—any more, and you're setting yourself up for failure (or a stay in the mental ward).

3. I THOUGHT YOU SAID FOOD WASN'T SO IMPORTANT, REALLY. CAN'T I JUST GET SOME NICE TAKEOUT?

We frown on passing off stuff from the Whole Foods salad bar as your own. But if you do need to buy prepared food as part of your dinner to ease the stress, then feel free. Eventually you'll realize that whatever you're buying is pretty easy to make, and you will probably make it taste better and spend less money while you're at it. We tend to buy premade things we couldn't ever make ourselves: really good cheeses, say, or the chickpea meth that is Sabra hummus.

4. I can't do this alone!

Nor should you. That 1963 horror *How to Give Successful Dinner Parties* advises an unmarried woman to "borrow" a friend's husband to act as host. This sounds a little pervy, and more than a bit dated, but the idea is solid: Hosting is better done in pairs. If you have no spouse/significant other/sex puppet who can chop vegetables, set the table and offer drinks (to you and to guests), just invite a friend. Or, better yet, invite someone you'd like to get to know better. Sharing a kitchen tends to break down defenses just as fast as, say, getting trapped in an avalanche, but it's much safer. And when you wildly succeed (as we know you will), you'll share your sense of accomplishment. We found each other through our shared love of cooking—who will you find?

Washing Up

Sunday Night Dinner took a huge step forward when Tamara started hiring a dishwasher, and you can use this same strategy for your own dinners if you feel like you might get overwhelmed. We're certainly glad to have the backup for twenty guests, but it can be a treat even if you're cooking for half that number. Guests are usually happy to chip in $5 or $10 apiece to get themselves off the cleanup hook. Tamara often pops by her local diner and asks if anyone there wants to make some easy money. We also draw on our friends—struggling artists, dancers and actors who'd rather drink wine and wash plates than sign up for another night of cater-waiting. Teenagers are a good bet too: Not only do they get cash, but they get to see the grownups make drunken fools of themselves.

5. Help! I don't have any furniture! Or silverware! Or . . . ! Or . . . !

Here's where it really pays to get creative. You're not alone if you don't have a dining room table—or even a dining room. Zora once threw a party without a table—she just called it an indoor picnic, laid out a tablecloth on the floor and made everyone sit around it.

Zora wouldn't, however, recommend this as your first course of action, unless you have really cushy carpeting. Otherwise, your guests' legs tend to fall asleep. That in itself is not so terrible, but Zora was also short on silverware for this party, and the same guest who got wedged in a weird corner and whose leg went totally numb also got stuck using a ladle as his only utensil. And, um, there weren't any dessert plates, so she just gave everyone a spoon and let people have at the lemon pudding. Unfortunately, Mr. Lame-Leg Ladle-Slurper fell behind while limping toward the feeding frenzy, and so he got the dessert shaft. Zora came out of the kitchen to find him sulking in a corner, sipping his wine from a mug (yeah, not enough glasses either). But it sure was a memorable dinner.

So let's address these problems one at a time.

Nowhere to sit? Go trash picking. Chairs are the most frequently tossed-out piece of furniture, usually because their owners got a newer, spiffier dining room set and the perfectly functional but frumpy ones were taking up space. If your city has big-item trash collection regularly, all you have to do is comb the streets on garbage night; smaller cities may require a little more planning ahead. In rural areas, head to the dump—at good dumps, thoughtful people will leave the desirable not-really-trash items up front, and you don't have to go pawing through anything.

Is this grossing you out? It shouldn't. People throw away incredibly useful stuff all the time. Just check for general structural soundness and for any obvious sticky stains—these attract bugs, and you of course don't want that. But the best part of pulling a chair out of your neighbor's trash is that you won't feel so bad about putting it right back out on the curb the day after your party. Think of your furniture as temporary only, and the solution becomes much easier.

In the same vein, you could also just ask your guests to bring their own chairs—call it potluck, but for your ass. We have done this numerous times, and in fact some guests have volunteered to bring their own chairs after we made them sit on a cinder block topped with a pillow or those tiny chairs we got at the 99-cents-and-more store. Folding chairs can get carted on the bus or subway, or tied to the back of your bike; comfier options fit just fine in a car trunk.

If you're short on space but would like something a bit more permanent, go for a bench or two—most of the time they'll sit off to the side collecting your mail, but they can be pressed into service at a moment's notice.

Setting up a table takes a bit more wherewithal. If you think you might really get into this cooking-for-friends thing but you have very little space, you could invest in a nifty folding table with matching chairs. Our friend Victoria has one of these—it looks like a tiny little sideboard when not in use but folds out to accommodate eight people and tons of Sicilian cooking (see Where to Get the Goods on page 228 for more).

Zora's a big fan of heroic furniture moving. Nothing says, "Oh boy, we're having a *party*!" like dragging all your bookcases, tchotchkes and armchairs into your bedroom (or hiding them behind the curtain that divides up your studio), just for the night. Ah—look how spacious your so-called living room finally is! You could dance in here! If you can't move the sofa, use it as seating for one side of the table, thus solving some of your chair issues at the same time. Your coffee table may also be the right height to be pressed into service as seating. If it looks like either situation will be a little low, add lots more pillows—and phone books, if necessary.

If you don't want to buy anything nicey-nice, look for other temporary solutions. Get the cheapest folding tables they have at Target. Or set up two sawhorses and top them with a door (also often salvageable from the trash); make sure no one leans too hard on one end. Instead of sawhorses, use your hopefully large coffee table as a base and stack books on top of it to bring it up to normal table height (36 inches). If you use a door from within your own home—preferably not the door to the bathroom, and make sure you or someone you know can put it back on its hinges when dinner is through—you will have indeed made something out of nothing.

OK, you've got some furniture. The rest of the stuff—plates, silverware, glasses, and so on—can all be answered with two words: Salvation Army. If you fancy yourself to have a bit more taste, then start prowling on eBay for secondhand silver-plate forks and knives. You can score a big box of mismatched utensils for $50 or so. Polish it up, and you will never need to get married just for the presents.

Thrift-shop the plates too, and don't bother getting matched sets. Zora was given an extensive collection of food-safe state plates, as well as one commemorating

Eisenhower's presidency. Chipped and faded and all different sizes, they don't really lend an aesthetic harmony to the table, but they are great conversation pieces. Over the years, she has also picked up some of her grandmother's not-so-fine china, some enamel-coated metal jobs from an African import store and even some plain white Ikea dinner plates.

For glassware, get creative. Save your empty jelly jars, for one thing. If you have a wild array of glassware, you won't need those gratuitous little "wine charms" to tell which drink is yours. You'll just need to look for the glass with Fred Flintstone on it.

We don't think we need to tell you that disposables are just not the way to go. We know, cleanup is a breeze, and Zora does have a fondness for those plastic sectional plates. But there's something so dispiriting about the scrape of plastic on plastic—it's like saying, "Hey, guests, you're just not worth the trouble." And you're sure to find that at least one of your guests genuinely likes doing the dishes—especially if you start a little dance party in the kitchen during this chore. (If you don't trust this will work, hire a dishwasher—see page 29.)

And this may sound a little extreme, but we also don't really go in for paper napkins. Cloth napkins (or dishtowels, or flour-sack cloths, or cheap washcloths, or even just a couple yards of cotton from the fabric store, snipped into squares with pinking shears) add an element of class that will make up for even the shoddiest assortment of tableware. Even when it looks like a shut-in schizophrenic set the table, guests all go "Oooooh!" as soon as you lay the cloth napkins at each place setting. And even *those* don't have to match! Moreover, they're reusable and subtly tell your friends that you care enough to do laundry for them.

6. HELP! I DON'T HAVE ANY FRIENDS!

Well, neither did we, until we started having people over for dinner. Some folks we've invited: Zora's mailman, the guy who runs the patisserie, a former priest, a Navy captain, the regular at the restaurant Tamara worked at, the surgeon who did Tamara's appendectomy, the French exchange student. . . . Frankly, it's amazing who will come when you're offering a home-cooked meal.

Shine a Light

You may not need matching dishes, but nice lighting is essential to making guests feel comfortable—it's about the only hostessing detail Zora gets really worked up about. There's something about the glare of overhead light that's soul-killing. Fortunately, the solution can be as easy as candles. With a couple of table or floor lamps (or leaving a light on in the kitchen), plus lots of candles on the table, you'll get a comfortable glow. Even candles alone are fine—your eyes will adjust. If your guests are clumsy, stick to tealights instead of teetery tapers (we test all holders for Karl-Proof Stability), and never use scented candles. Another nice thing about candlelight: No one will notice if you drop your dinner on your shirt.

It's also amazing that none of these people turned out to be an axe murderer. Or even a petty thief. Everyone we've invited into our homes has turned out to be baseline decent, and that's not because we're good judges of character. It's because people, as long as they aren't junkies short on cash, *are* baseline decent. Actually, it's a bit more self-selecting than that: People who think it would be nice to sit around your house while you feed them dinner and ply them with wine are baseline decent. It's the people who get the invitation and say, "Gee, thanks, but I have this PR party with an open bar and some catalog models to go to that night" that you probably have to worry about—and what luck, they're not coming!

Also keep in mind that a few strangers—or at least friends of friends—at a party will help get the conversation going. A group of twenty can easily absorb three wild cards, and a group of ten can handle one or two.

Some people are apprehensive even about inviting known friends over. Perhaps still nursing a grade-school birthday party trauma, you may have that creeping fear that no one will come, and you'll be left sitting alone at the table with congealing pasta and wilting lettuce. We hear that. It's not like we were throwing brilliant bashes back in fifth grade either. But we're all adults now, and we just have to trust that our friends are truly decent enough to show up for dinner (c'mon— free food!). And if they don't (but, really, they *will*)—well, fuck 'em. They are terrible friends, and it is *not your fault.* Save the leftover pasta for tomorrow, and go get some new friends. See the beginning of this section for tips.

7. WHAT ELSE AM I FORGETTING?

Well, missy, have you scrubbed the baseboards with bleach? Do your windowsills pass the white-glove test? Have you arranged the matching shams just so atop your freshly made bed? Oh, wait—that was Tamara's mother talking. We're here to tell you, contrary to all parental advice and Christian aphorisms, that you absolutely do *not* have to clean your apartment before company comes. Of course it's only polite to pick up your dirty clothes and gather last week's newspapers into a stack (and maybe put your guilty-pleasure copy of *Us Weekly* in the bathroom, where everyone can flip through it), but if your guests are really looking in the corners for dust bunnies, they're probably not your real friends anyway—or you haven't given them enough to drink. Tamara swears she had an epiphany the first time she came over to dinner at Peter's, and it was pretty damn clear that he hadn't cleaned the bathroom before she arrived. "You can *do* that?" Tamara stood there thinking, as her Austrian blood rushed to her head. Since then, Tamara has really let things slide—although she always makes sure there's plenty of toilet paper on hand, and she generally doesn't take off her bra and toss it over a doorknob till near the end of the night.

 Everybody Polka!

When you're cooking and entertaining, pick music that you love, "good taste" and "ambience" be damned. You will be happier and more relaxed if you're working to your favorite tunes, and your guests will appreciate that they're not hearing the standard mood music du jour.

CHAPTER 3

PREP: THE FOOD! THE SHOPPING!

S o just what will you cook, and how will you cook it? Given the glut of ingredients available in supermarkets and the number of cookbooks on store shelves, this is one of the more perplexing problems for a newish cook.

We'll first lay out the gear you'll need to get up and running in your kitchen, and then talk you through the process of deciding what to cook. Once that's settled, we'll head out on a predinner shopping trip. And if you've been wondering what a boner is, there's a glossary of terms and techniques at the end, plus tips for wielding a knife.

WHAT A WELL-STOCKED KITCHEN DOES (AND DOESN'T) NEED

Some people, when they take up a new activity, go out and buy all the doodads for it all at once, perhaps thinking that the cash outlay will motivate them to use their new superhero titanium bike, their featherweight helmet, their form-fitting spandex shorts and so on. If this strategy actually works for you, fine.

But it's easier on your wallet, and on your kitchen's storage space, if you start out with the bare minimum of gear. If, after a year of cooking, you're still dying for that cherry pitter, then go for it. But in general, you want to avoid having a drawer that's a graveyard for unloved kitchen gadgets.

With this in mind, it should be easy to avoid Williams-Sonoma completely. Cake pans shaped like adorable German villages, silicone-coated whisks, flower-shaped pancake molds—you don't need any of that business. In particular, multipiece sets of cookware are one of the biggest scams around, especially when they're endorsed by some celeb chef or other.

What you do need:

- **A cast-iron skillet—or two.** Cast iron is for some reason unloved today, perhaps because Americans have grown too feeble to lift the stuff. They're also afraid of somehow damaging the mysterious "seasoning" on the pan. (For years, Zora thought "seasoning" had something to do with spices. She was relieved when she learned it's really just baked-on grease.) And, yes, there is the legitimate issue that long-simmering acidic foods, such as wine or tomatoes, will cause a reaction with the metal and perhaps create a weird flavor.

  But cast iron is sturdy and, when properly cared for, totally non-stick, and it crisps the crusts on cornbread and fried chicken like nothing else. Plus, it's cheap: You can pick up an old one in an antiques shop for $10—such a good deal that you may find yourself adopting too many, as Zora and Peter have. An excellent new "preseasoned" skillet goes for about $20. The best all-purpose ones are biggish (9 or 10 inches) with deep sides and a lip for pouring. A smaller one is useful, though not required, for frying eggs. Try also to get one with a smooth handle—some newer ones have an irritating seam along the edge, from the mold. Also look around for a lid—Zora has a heavy tempered-glass one, but use whatever you can rustle up that fits reasonably well.

- **Big stainless-steel pot with a lid.** For boiling pasta, steaming vegetables or making soup or stock, you need something with an 8-quart capacity. It should come with a tight-fitting lid. Zora's is a $30 Farberware stainless-steel job, but you could conceivably splurge on a pricier pot with a thicker bottom so you can also simmer soups with less risk of scorching, as well as tomato sauces (which you shouldn't do for more than, say, half an hour in a cast-iron skillet).

Give Your Skillet a Lick of Love

Cast-iron skillets require only a little special attention, and when you give it, they will flourish into glossy, black, nonstick things of beauty. Wash them as soon as possible after cooking in them, to keep flavors from soaking in and food from glomming on. They usually just need a rinse and a quick wipe with a sponge. Purists say not to use any soap, but if there happens to be some in the sponge you're using, it won't be a disaster. Then set the skillet back on the stove over a low flame to dry (and, er, remember to turn off the burner when you're done), to prevent rust. Also, "I'll just let this soak" is not the best strategy for cast iron, as the standing water eats away the seasoning. But if your pan does wind up looking sickly and wan, you can restore the finish through the traditional miracle cure: bacon. Fry up half a pound, and your skillet will be back at peak performance in no time.

- **Some sort of midsize saucepan.** This one you definitely want to have a heavier bottom. Think of it as a safety cushion—it will save a distracted cook from many scorching disasters. Zora has a groovy orange Descoware enamel-coated cast-iron pan, but a stainless-steel design with an aluminum core is a little lighter, heats more evenly and won't react with acidic ingredients. Nonstick is irrelevant here—you won't be doing anything in this pan that will really bake on.

- **Dutch oven.** This used to refer to a specific shape of pot, but the term now often refers to any heavy large pot (5–8 quarts) with a lid. Enameled cast iron is expensive but ideal for this, if you're going to be doing any regular roasting, braising, deep-frying or soup making for more than a few people (and, because you're reading this book, we imagine you will be). But start first with just your skillets and pasta pot, and keep an eye out for sales on Le Creuset, or, if you're lucky, vintage Descoware and other old brands.

Sharing Is Caring

As we're situated by some excellent grocery stores, we don't pop over to the neighbor's to borrow a cup of sugar—but we do get all Donna Reed when it comes to pots and pans. Want to make cassoulet but don't have a pot that's big enough? Call a friend who does. There's no need for everyone in your circle to be stocked to the gills with cookware. When you pool resources, you have not only a better-stocked kitchen, but stronger friendships too!

- **Three knives.** And *only* three knives. Sharp, glittery and misused in countless horror films, kitchen knives can strike fear in the novice cook—but you need to get over that. Wielded well, a knife is a simple machine that does your work for you. You'll want a 10-inch chef's knife, a long serrated blade for bread and tomatoes and a small paring knife. Only the chef's knife has to be good quality, and even then, you can start with a cheap one, just to get the feel of it, and upgrade later.

- **Knife sharpener.** When you get a quality blade, also buy some tool for keeping it sharp—a line cook samurai will tell you that an electric knife sharpener (like Zora's Chef's Choice model) is for wimps, but we sure do enjoy freshly honed blades at the drop of a hat. And if you spring for one of these gadgets, you can charm your friends and neighbors by offering to sharpen their knives as well. Funny, Samurai Dude has never offered to sharpen our knives by hand. We feel duty-bound to say it's nice to have a sharpening steel—those long, pointy things that you always see TV chefs whisking their knives along before they get down to business—but, frankly, we get along without one just fine.

- **Large wood cutting board.** Nothing is more of a pain in the ass than having to cut things up in a very small space. If you have a tiny counter, order a slab of butcher block (The Home Depot sells it by the square foot) to fit part of it. Wipe the board down religiously and moisturize it with mineral oil every few months, and you'll have a forgiving, hygienic and durable cutting surface.

- **Wooden spoons.** They're cheap—get a few. One with a flat bottom edge is handy for stirring sauces.

- **Silicone spatulas.** Also not too expensive, and very handy. If you really, really want to buy something from Williams-Sonoma, it could be these. Get a small one and a large one—and then use them. A well-scraped pan is that much easier to wash.

- **Tongs.** Good for pulling chickens out of ovens or scooping asparagus out of boiling water. Start with a standard pair, then invest in a super-long set for grilling later.

- **Colander.** You don't realize you need one until you've got a big pot of hot liquid that needs straining. Get a metal one, so you can wear it on your head to keep the alien rays out. Or use a fine-mesh strainer, which can double as a flour sieve.

- **Stainless-steel bowls.** Lightweight and versatile, for tossing salads, mixing pasta with sauce and more. Get at least one very big one to start. But they're stackable and extremely cheap, so why not get three or four?

A metal colander is a sensible investment.

- **Baking sheet.** Don't get one with a nonstick finish—not just probably toxic, but also requiring finicky nonmetal tools. And you want your cookies to brown, right?

- **Microplane grater.** Handy for hard cheeses, lemon peel and fresh nutmeg.

- **Salad spinner.** When Zora was growing up, it was often her job to wash and dry the lettuce for the salad—every night, by hand. She didn't even know salad spinners existed. Although it's a loving gesture to pat each leaf of lettuce dry with a clean dish towel, it's also the sort of thing that's only sustainable through child labor. So the salad spinner is brilliant for single people, but optional for those who have kids.

- **Garlic press.** For some people—especially those with flawless knife skills—this veers into unnecessary gadgetry. But for mere mortals, it's the easiest way to mash up a clove of garlic for your salad dressing, and for that alone it's essential. There are loads of crappily designed garlic presses on the market, though—to be safe, get a Swiss-made Zussi model. An additional tip: Zora was astonished to learn—again, after years of exploitative labor—that you can actually drop garlic cloves into the press *without peeling them.*

That's it. If you start cooking for more people more often, you'll want to expand your collection of pots and pans. If you do a lot of sauces, a whisk is nice. If you do a lot of baking, of course that's a whole world of sifters and cake pans to get into. And chances are, you'll find yet another good cast-iron skillet that's just begging to be adopted.

Zora's batterie de cuisine,

heavy on the cast iron

WHAT TO COOK (AND WHAT NOT TO)

Deciding what to cook is the single biggest hurdle to actually cooking. For our big dinners, we sit around hemming and hawing over the menu, flipping idly through cookbooks and waiting for inspiration to strike. More often than not, though, we wind up first ruling out what we *won't* cook. The weather helps do this (grilled anything seems depressing when it's 55°F and cloudy), but more important, the seasons dictate what we'll eat.

We're not going to cane you for buying fresh raspberries in January—we've done it ourselves—but paying attention to what's in season is the easiest way to narrow down the absurdly huge field of things an American with access to a decent grocery store can cook on any given night. If it's April, dig out the asparagus recipes and boil as many artichokes as you can; if it's August, gorge on tomatoes; in the winter, get your fill of butternut squash.

It can be hard in a contemporary American supermarket to even tell what *should* be in season, but learning this stuff pays off—literally, because seasonal produce is usually cheaper than something shipped from Chile. As a bonus, if you stuff yourself full of certain items when they're in season, you'll be good and sick of them for a while, and less likely to crave them at impractical times of the year. Stop by your farmers' market every so often just to see what's for sale—you can buy there, or then look for the same items in the grocery store, where they're also likely to be on special.

The ideal, of course, is to ramble over to the farmers' market, pick through all the piles of fresh-from-the-earth vegetables, stuff the best ones in your string bags and then ride your bicycle home like the European you wish you were. If you have the confidence to bring home ingredients and wing it, then by all means do it—but most people will have to start cooking by finding recipes that look good, making a list of ingredients, hunting them down at the fluorescent-lit megamart and hoping they haven't forgotten something when they get home.

Which brings us back to the problem of how to choose a recipe. Once you've ruled out the obvious seasonal mismatches, this is still a complicated business, based on your skill level, the time you have and how the stars are aligned as you're flipping through the cookbooks or magazines. But the easiest guide is to *pick something you're hungry for.* It seems obvious, sure, but too often we pick something we think we *should* eat, or something we think will impress someone else. If you have picky eaters in your family or circle of friends, tell them they just have to be a little more flexible. Being the cook is like being the driver: You get to choose the music (in the car *or* the kitchen), and you get to decide what people are going to eat.

The best part about picking a recipe that satisfies a craving, and then cooking it, is that you'll feel totally godlike. It's an exciting thing to discover that it is within your power to make pizza, for instance. Or pasta. Or even a good salad dressing. For Zora, that *aha!* moment came with making mashed potatoes for the first time—in her house, they'd been solely a Christmas-and-Thanksgiving food. But when she learned how easy they were to make, she saw no reason why she couldn't have them all the time.

Your Kitchen, Your Choice

In this age of low-carb diets and gluten sensitivities, fill a room with ten people and chances are, you'll get a laundry list of preferences/allergies if you ask: vegetarian, vegan, no fats, no salt, no dairy because it gives me zits. . . . What's a fledgling host(ess) to do? Simple: *Don't ask.* If you have a couple of vegetarians in the crowd, make sure you have plenty of vegetable sides and subtly let them know by giving the menu out in the invitation. Your guests won't die or have a horrible time if they don't get to eat one of the dishes—we know from experience. Tamara hates carrots, sweet potatoes and winter squash, while Zora cannot abide cooked bell peppers. Does this mean we decline all invites that include these items? Hell, no! We politely pass on the dish(es) as they go around the table, and eat more of what we *do* like. No one is the wiser because we *keep our mouths shut about it* (just one example of how old-fashioned manners can improve our daily lives). That said, an all-pork menu for your new Jewish or Muslim sweetie's family is perhaps not advisable, but with a little knowledge of your guests and an ability to prioritize the actual deadly allergy versus the "cilantro tastes like soap to me" objections, you'll be fine.

Scooby Snacks—Serve 'Em

After one too many way-behind-schedule dinners where guests spent three hours boozing it up while we pulled together our latest magnum opus, we got serious about planning a little snacky treat to be ready when guests arrive: a couple of good cheeses, fresh figs, spicy nuts or radishes with butter and salt. With this small gesture, we now keep the impatient hordes out of the kitchen, and also just sober enough to converse once they finally sit down. Plus, glassware breakage has decreased significantly, and we hardly ever get e-mails the next day from people apologizing for their inappropriate behavior.

Once you've settled on a single hankering—for lasagna, for instance—you also need to figure out how to round that into a meal. Try to avoid what we call postcollege bachelor(ette) cooking, in which you cook a giant one-pot dish, often involving lentils because they're cheap, and then eat it for days on end, until you get totally sick of it and toss the remaining two portions in the garbage. Not only is this no fun to serve to guests, but it's also a waste of your good cooking efforts. It's just plain boring to eat one thing, and you'll wind up wondering why you went to the trouble.

Even though the phrase "one-pot meal" is bandied about all over the place, it's just not a full meal unless there's a little something on the side, so to speak. Even the best soup will leave you wanting something else, but serve it with a light salad and maybe a little bread, and you've got enough to keep your palate entertained through the meal.

But if you're cooking more than one thing, that means—ack!—you have to pick out yet another recipe from the bazillions ever written. Again, start by ruling things out. Avoid overlapping flavors—if there's basil in the pasta, don't make a basil salad dressing—and also think about how the colors and textures will go together, which, incidentally, will help you get a good mix of nutrients as well. If you want to serve both sweet potatoes and red cabbage (a great color combo), consider

Count Your Pots and Burners

For a dinner of chicken-fried steak, Tamara once chose four other stove-top recipes. But she didn't realize her miscalculation until she'd already dedicated two of her four flames to the steak. Dinner was a bit late that night. (On the plus side, she did discover—through a shortage of large pots—that you can boil asparagus and then poach eggs in the same water. The eggs turn only faintly green.) So mix up your menu: Have some stove-top dishes, and some that can be tucked away in the oven. Better yet, plan on a few dishes that don't need to be piping hot when they hit the table—these can be done first and set aside, ideally at room temperature, so your fridge doesn't suffer overload as well. And always remember that you probably have only one pot big enough for boiling veggies.

serving the cabbage as a raw, crispy slaw, to contrast with the soft potatoes. If you're roasting some fatty duck, pair it with plain steamed greens—bitter ones, like escarole, are especially good. And for a simple weeknight meal, apply Zora's mother's rule: Always have something green on the plate—even if it's just frozen peas.

Finally, go light on the meat. This isn't just a health issue—it's also a budgetary one. Maybe no one throws dinner parties anymore because so many recipes call for two quails in an entrée portion, or an 8-ounce filet mignon. Preportioned food like this is an evil, let's-pretend-we're-at-a-restaurant trap—not everyone wants to eat two whole birds, or a giant slab of beef, but as a host, you don't want to look chintzy. Believe us, there are plenty of ways to be chintzy and never, ever let your guests know! You'll wind up cooking far more delicious and interesting things for far less money if you opt not for steak (everyone already knows what that tastes like) but for something like a braised pork shoulder, from which each person can serve themselves the portion they prefer. And a giant hunk of one thing looks much grander on the table than twee little plated bits. Even when we do lamb shanks or duck legs, we leave them all in the roasting pan on the table and let people dig out the amount of meat that looks good to them—it's like a self-created loaves-and-fishes miracle. We've heard that the trendy word for this kind of cooking (that is, making cheap meat taste amazing) is "rustic"—lucky for us, humans have been cooking "rustically" for thousands of years, so there's a lot of collected wisdom to draw on.

And meat doesn't even have to be the centerpiece. In fact, it's a lot easier, as well as better for you, if it's not. Though we'll often think first of something mammoth like a leg of lamb (or a whole beast, for that matter), we usually end up getting much more excited about all the side dishes, which are usually a cinch to put together. And the more side dishes you cook, the less meat there needs to be. Taking this to its logical conclusion, you can wind up with a meatless meal, and that's perfectly legit, even if you and your friends don't happen to be avowed vegetarians. The only time Zora has ever been reprimanded for this was in Egypt, where she cooked a huge spread of Indian dishes for some friends. One of the guests said, "That's nice, but where's the meat?" In fact, she'd been so fascinated by all the new flavor combinations she was trying out, she hadn't even realized there wouldn't be any meat. Never feel shame for not serving meat—this is something that, at least in the United States, is just a bad hangover from our grandmothers' generation.

Don't Plan a Menu When You're Starving

Even culinary masterminds like ourselves can make some bad choices when we head to the grocery store on an empty stomach. One cold wintry night, Zora found herself at the checkout counter with ingredients for both lasagna and mac and cheese, and no vegetables in sight. Overexcited by a new cookbook, Tamara dashed out for the fixings for three different starches (couscous, potatoes and cranberry beans). We now try to do our menu fantasizing right after lunch, or have some cheese and crackers on hand while we're thinking.

Go get 'em, tiger!

You've got your menu sorted, you've got your kitchen gear. . . . Now it's time to actually invite people over and stock the house. Try to invite people at least a week before dinner; if you live a high-powered city life, it may have to be further ahead than that. But don't give *too* much notice, as that leaves time for pressure and unreasonable expectations to build.

After that, don't sit by your laptop, hitting refresh on your e-mail. Start making lists. Depending on your personality, this is where the whole dinner party project gets either tedious or gratifying. If you're Tamara, the mere mention of a list makes you feel like you've been locked in jail. If you're Zora, making a list soothes the nerves and keeps the world spinning on its axis. In truth, Tamara has actually come around to list making over the years, after she made one too many same-day trips to the grocery store.

Identify any odd or exotic ingredients first and head out for an exploratory shop the weekend before your party. If you can't find what's on your list—or if you find something even more delicious-looking—you still have time to adjust your menu. And if you happen to see any nonperishable items you know you'll need, pick up those too, just to get a jump on things. Also stop in at your butcher and make sure you'll be able to get whatever you need the following weekend. If you don't have a butcher, at least check out the meat case in the supermarket and make sure the various cuts you need are there—and if they're not, you'll be able to figure out a suitable alternative.

If your party's going to be on a Saturday, do a quick shop on Wednesday or Thursday for all your pantry items, plus milk, eggs and the like. Also pick up any wine or other drinks you're planning. If you'll be cooking meat that needs defrosting, buy it today and let it thaw in the fridge over the next couple of days. And if your menu requires ripe fruit, pick it up on this trip too—assuming you're dealing with normal, less-than-prime supermarket fruit. Set it out on the counter or wrap it up in a paper bag to ripen over the next few days.

On Friday evening or Saturday morning, make a second shopping run for your vegetables, any additional fruit and your meat, if you haven't gotten it already. Buy some ice if you think you'll need it.

Keep It at Eye Level

Whenever we cook, we combine recipes from all over to create a single menu. This requires a lot of consultation of various cookbooks, newspaper clippings and each other's memories—all of which has often led to panic, confusion and occasional crankiness at some point during the cooking. On a couple of occasions, we've just plain forgotten about an entire dish (after-dinner revelation: "Fuck! The kale!"). Now we avoid that moment when we're standing in the middle of the kitchen, all four burners blazing, looking around and mumbling, "What next?" We copy or print out the recipes we're using and tape them up on our kitchen cabinets, at eye level, where we both can see them—no more lost scraps of paper or books hidden under piles of produce. And now that Tamara's a fan of lists, she usually tapes her prep list up as well, where she can keep track of the progress we're making.

Just a warning: If you're not in the habit of cooking regularly and your cupboards are totally bare, you're going to be a little appalled at the amount of money you spend shopping for a dinner. Resist the urge to calculate how many cheeseburgers $120 could buy. This is a fallacy. In the long run, it's all money well spent. Spices may cost $3 or $5 for a jar, but you'll be using them for the next year. A few months from now, you'll be able to look in your cabinet and see that you already have half the ingredients for a given dish, rather than none.

Once you get all your booty home, take good care of it. Vegetables should all be wrapped loosely in plastic bags to prevent wilting, for instance, and if they're wet, toss a paper towel in the bag to absorb the moisture and keep it off the leaves. If you have hungry roommates or curious family members, tell them explicitly what to keep their mitts off. And always do a quick inventory before you start cooking on the day of the party—as one wise chef once told Tamara and Zora, "if you don't put your hand on it an hour before you need it, it may as well be gone." Oh, and make sure you have a corkscrew—you'll need it.

Resist the urge to start cooking right away—once you get into the kitchen, it's hard to get out. First, pick up all your junk mail and sweep the dust bunnies under the rug, then do any ambitious furniture moving you may have planned. Collect the plates and silverware you'll be using, but don't lay them out. Setting the table is a great task for any dreaded early-arriving guests—it makes them feel useful and gets them out of your hair.

Once you get into the kitchen, take a few minutes to clear the decks—advice we wish we could always heed ourselves, as we're usually too excited or panicked and jump right in. (As a result, whenever Zora arrives at Tamara's—and vice versa—she usually spends about ten minutes tidying up around the already frenziedly cooking Tamara.) Group together ingredients for each dish; pile them on your counter if you have space, or put them in separate shopping bags.

For all the menus in this book, we've outlined a plan of attack—what tasks you should start first and which you can leave till closer to dinnertime. Follow the plan, and you should get everything done roughly at the same time.

ESSENTIAL COOKING TERMS, TECHNIQUES AND INGREDIENTS

Posh Nosh tells you to "excite" your chicken and "fan-base" your garnishes—they're making that shit up, obviously, but sometimes the real terminology can be just as absurd and opaque. Here's what you really need to know:

Boner: Get your mind out of the gutter! We mean a boning knife. This thin, flexible blade can be very handy once you get into, well, boning. (OK, we admit we put this word in the glossary just because we think it's funny.)

Braise: The way you should cook meat, and some veggies, all winter long—basically a Crock-Pot, but using your own pot. Standard operating procedure is to brown your meat in a Dutch oven (or your cast-iron skillet with a lid, or your heavy-bottomed stockpot), add your vegetables and whatever herbs or spices and pour in stock and/or wine to fill about a third of the way up the meat. Put on the lid, stick that baby in the oven at 300°F and go back to reading the newspaper for the next few hours. If you want something braised for dinner on a weeknight, set the oven even lower—225°F or 250°F—and leave the dish in there for the day. Or, if you're afraid the house will burn down in your absence, do the prep the night before and leave the pot in till morning, as we advise in the chuck roast recipe on page 122. We haven't yet died in our sleep from doing this, and it really feels effortless if you can actually snooze while you're "cooking." As a bonus, braised dishes always taste better if they're prepared ahead, chilled and then reheated. We don't know why—maybe the smug satisfaction of having done no work makes them taste better.

Butter: Embrace it. You cannot use margarine instead. You cannot use Hypermodern Heart-Lovers Butterish Goo. Butter makes a lot of things taste good, and it is far better for you than any nasty invented faux fat— our excellent cholesterol counts are proof. Throughout this book, we don't specify salted or unsalted butter because you should be adding salt to your taste as you go—and you should never be running out to the store just to get the "right" butter for a recipe.

Deglaze: Get those yummy browned bits of meat off the bottom of the pan and into your sauce or braising liquid by keeping the heat on medium-high and pouring in a small amount of wine or stock, then scraping quickly as the pan sizzles and steams. Repeat as necessary. Incidentally, you can use the same technique for cleaning baked-on nastiness off pots, substituting soapy water for wine.

Dice: To cut something into small, even cubes; a synonym for *as if.* If a recipe says "dice an onion," a larger, lazier chopping job will almost certainly be just fine. In our kitchen, *dice* refers only to craps, Tamara's favorite casino game.

Peeling Is Overrated

Tamara spent hours peeling potatoes and apples for her parents as a child—and now she has rebelled. She will probably never peel another piece of fruit or a potato unless the Queen Mother comes back from the dead and wants to dine. Honestly, we think you have bigger fish to fry than to worry about peeling anything—we safely ignore instructions to do so in most recipes. Not only do we save time, but we get added texture and visual contrast, plus extra nutrients and flavor. Just be sure to wash your fruit or veggies very thoroughly, and you're good to go!

Double boiler: One of the world's more useless, finicky kitchen items. If a recipe calls for a double boiler (one pot set above another filled with boiling water), you know you're in either culinary fantasyland or super-remedial cooking classes. Proceed with skepticism, and just do what we do: Use a plain old heavy-bottomed skillet or pot, directly over very low heat—then pay close attention and stir like a mofo.

Fat: "Fat is flavor" is the mantra of many pro cooks, and they're right. We're not saying you have to slather everything in grease, but if you have any lingering fear of much-maligned lard, duck fat, schmaltz or butter, get over it. A judicious dab of duck fat will leave your guests staggering with joy, and it's actually good for you. Which is not to say animal fat is the definitive best—there are many situations in which good olive oil shines, and you should invest in a good bottle (or a 3-liter tin).

Fold: Karl recently mentioned that he'd finally understood this term only a couple of years ago, so we mention it here. Usually recipes instruct you to fold fluffy egg whites into something else, like a cake batter. This means you put a big blob of the egg whites on top of the batter, then reach down to the bottom of the bowl with a big wide spatula and lift the batter up and gently over the whites. Imagine you're wrapping the egg whites up in the batter, like a Christmas present.

Fry: To cook something in a lot of fat. Pan-frying means whatever you're frying is about half-covered in fat; with deep-frying, there's enough fat in the pan to fully dunk if you need to (though whatever you're frying will float in the oil and need to be flipped anyway). Frying is intimidating for novices, mostly because it's messy and has a reputation as being unhealthy. Well, it's kind of true, but frying is kitchen alchemy at its best: Pop a dollop of batter in some oil, then pull out a golden fritter and watch your guests pass out with delight—now that's magic. To clean up after the frying frenzy, set the oil aside to cool completely, then pour it back into its old container and chuck it. If it's a smaller amount, pour it into a coffee or tomato can and stick it in the freezer, then chuck it when it's solid. (Never, ever pour grease down your sink drain, unless you hate your landlord and are planning to move soon anyway.) You can reuse deep-fry oil if it didn't get smoking-hot on the first outing; strain out the burned bits from the previous batch and keep it covered.

Mandoline: Even ex–police officer Peter, who sees nothing wrong with boozing while carrying a loaded gun, says, "Mandolines are dangerous!" This nifty flat device promises speedy, paper-thin slices—often at the cost of a fingertip, if you're not paying attention. If a recipe casually instructs you to use one of these, it's a good indicator that the person who wrote it is insane. We'd never ask such a thing of you—better to learn to use your chef's knife confidently and efficiently.

Poach: Nothing to do with killing endangered animals, but simply cooking in just enough liquid to cover. Poaching is most commonly associated with eggs, to produce a luscious runny yolk. (Incidentally, we find it completely gross that it's now not considered safe to eat a partially cooked egg. It behooves you to spend the extra two bucks to buy organic. Think of it as a bit of insurance against industrial farming's salmonella-spewing practices.) But it's also a lot more versatile than that: You can also simmer meat, fish, vegetables or fruit in water—or

War Wounds

We have to warn you: You're going to get hurt in the kitchen. Not just the kind of heartbreak that comes from having your soufflé fall, but actual flesh wounds. When it comes to kitchen injuries, you're either a burner or a cutter. Zora's a born burner: At age three, she scorched her leg with hot bacon grease, and the singed flesh hasn't stopped since. Easily distracted, mandoline-loving Tamara is prone to cutting herself. The payback for all of these injuries is not only serious respec' from other cooks, but also undeniable appeal to the opposite sex. "Scars are *hawt,*" Peter leers at Zora every time she burns herself. On the other hand, whining is not sexy—so you just have to slather on some aloe and a Band-Aid and get back in the game. (Nor, for that matter, is spurting blood sexy—a hospital may be called for in that case.)

broth, stock, sugar syrup or olive oil. You can even poach something like salmon in duck fat!

Preheat: Most people know to turn on the oven well before they slide their tray of brownies in. Fewer know to preheat pans as well. Set them on the burner and let them warm up before adding anything—including oil—and your food is much less likely to stick.

Salt: Often overlooked by novice cooks, salt is key to making things—even sweet things—taste good. We use kosher salt exclusively. It's not because it tastes better, but because it's easier to work with. Pinch for pinch, it's not quite as salty as regular fine-grain table salt, so it gives you a little leeway. And the big flakes are more visible when you toss them in or on something, so you can keep better track of how much you're adding. We use Diamond (in the black-and-red box); the bigger flakes of Morton's kosher salt are a little extreme. (Don't worry—you won't get a goiter going without the iodine.) The few precise salt measurements in this cookbook are for Diamond kosher salt; if you have only table salt, use a bit less.

Sauté: Sounds fancy and French, but it just means to cook food in a wide pan with a little bit of fat. Unless you have a 60,000-Btu burner, there's no need to stir crazily while you're sautéing—in fact, letting your food sit still in the pan for a bit gives it time to brown, which is what you want to happen.

Spatchcock: Another word we put in just because we like saying it. This is the process of cutting the backbone out of a chicken (or any bird) and flattening the carcass out, so the bird cooks faster and more evenly. I guess we have to also tell you that *spatchcocking* is a British term; *butterflying* is what they call it in the United States. *Bo*-ring.

Ventilation: Your kitchen requires it—or else you'll be scrambling to unplug the smoke alarm every time you fry bacon. Most range hood fans do absolutely nothing except suck the greasy air up from the stove and blast it out into the kitchen, dispersing the grease in a fine haze. So get a sturdy box fan and set it in the window with the blades blowing out.

Wine: The secret ingredient in so many things. And don't worry about using cheap stuff you wouldn't ordinarily drink (but maybe it's easy for us to say that, because we have nothing against a $6 bottle of Spanish red) or something that's (somehow) left over from dinner a night or two before. If wine *in* the dish has failed to perk it up, wine administered directly to guests will certainly do the trick.

Feeling overwhelmed? Lists and glossaries can do that. No one expects you to retain all this information the first time around. Reward yourself for getting this far by pouring yourself a glass of wine.

Now get cooking—start with the very basic menu in the next chapter, or skip ahead to our suggestions for manageable menus based on seasonal ingredients. Just don't flip to the back—that's where the scary and dangerously tempting stuff is. . . .

Mad Knife Skillz

Long ago, moms taught daughters to slice carrots in their hands, pressing a dull knife through the veg and into their thumb. Then macho restaurant dudes whipped out their mini-swords (no coincidence that 10 inches is the measurement for a chef's knife) and developed more efficient techniques for slicing and dicing. As much as our hearts are with the home-cooking matriarchy, we are impressed by someone who can slice an onion in three seconds—even if he is wearing chili pepper pants.

You can be a good cook and still clomp your knife all over the board, Tamara is living proof. But learning basic skills will make your life easier and make you feel like a bad-ass. Start with these two ways for dealing with an onion, and make sure your knife is sharp. For better control, place your thumb and index finger right on the base of the blade.

Pole-to-Pole Slices

This is the most versatile way to slice up an onion, producing curved arcs of onion that can be paper-thin (for salads, for instance) or thicker (for caramelized onions or rice pilaf). The technique is a modified version of culinary-school textbook onion slicing, which focuses more on anally perfect slices than speed. We prefer speed.

1. Slice both ends off the onion.

2. Slice lengthwise through the outermost layer of the onion (no prob if you cut a little deeper by mistake), then peel off the outer layer and discard it.

3. Slice the onion in half lengthwise.

4. Holding half of the onion with a clawlike grip, start slicing from pole to pole, from right to left (if you're right-handed). Don't start

slicing straight down, but cut in from the side, following the natural curve of the onion.

5. When you get about two-thirds of the way through and the onion is getting hard to balance, tip it over on its side and continue slicing.

6. Repeat with the second onion half.

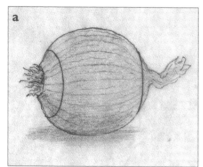

Slice both ends off the onion.

Slice into the outermost layer to remove the peel.

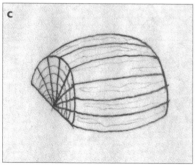

Pole-to-pole slices: cut lengthwise at an angle . . .

. . . tipping the last portion over to finish.

Rough Chop

Probably unsanctioned by "official" culinary technique, this is nonetheless the easiest way to get coarse chunks of onion, which are useful in just about every instance where long slices are not. (We'll never ask you to do it, but if for some reason you need finely chopped onion, do the pole-to-pole slices, then turn them sideways and chop fine across.)

1. Prep the onion through step 3 as for pole-to-pole slices.

2. Holding the onion on either side between your thumb and middle finger, make three or four lengthwise slices, depending on the size of the onion. Use the top of your index finger to hold the cut sections in place while you pull the knife through.

3. Still holding the slices together, but now with your hand turned sideways and your fingers out of the way, slice crosswise, to make large squares.

4. Repeat with the second onion half.

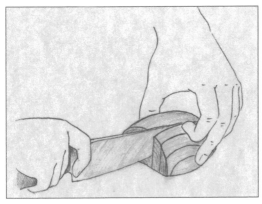

Rough chop: Make thick lengthwise slices straight down . . .

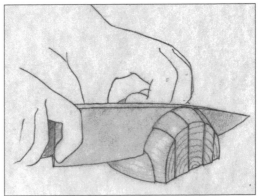

. . . then turn onion and slice crosswise.

CHAPTER 4

A DRY RUN

We don't really believe you need this chapter. (We have faith in you, dear readers! We expect great things!) But everyone else seemed pretty nervous at the prospect of just dumping you right into the flames of the next section of the book. So consider the following a dinner party with training wheels, for those of you who are really, *really* new to this whole "cooking" idea. We'll do a step-by-step walk-through of one of the most basic dinner party menus, a straightforward one with ingredients you can get anywhere, any time of year.

BABY-STEP DINNER PARTY

- Roast Chicken with Potatoes
- Green Salad
- Baked Apples

If you're looking at that menu and yawning, that's fair. We wrote it boring like that on purpose, to illustrate an essential lesson: Good cooking doesn't come from fancy, trendy ingredients that sound titillating (bottarga! pheasant! microgreens!). It happens when you treat basic ingredients well and serve them with love. And whenever interviewers ask fancy chefs what they prefer to cook at home, they *always* say roast chicken—probably because the crispy skin is one of the world's finest taste sensations.

But we're not making you cook something totally bland. The chicken gets a kick from lemon and garlic, the salad has a homemade vinaigrette and a couple of not-typical trimmings and the baked apples will make your house smell terrific. All the recipes we describe here serve four—a good starter number for guests or practicing on your family—but can be multiplied with ease and no change in proportions.

Plan of Attack

1. Set chicken out to get the fridge chill off—nice if you think of it about an hour before you start cooking.

2. Preheat oven.

3. Prep chicken and potatoes and put in to roast.

4. Prep salad; stow in fridge.

5. Toast croutons, if using.

6. Make salad dressing.

7. Prep apples. Put these in to bake when you remove the chicken.

8. While chicken is resting, dress salad and make sure there's wine, water, utensils, napkins and so forth on the table.

9. Sit down and enjoy dinner. Apples will coincidentally be done just around the time you're finishing.

Drink Up!

Tamara grew up watching Marilyn Monroe movies and thinking that every occasion was perfect for Champagne. Imagine her surprise as a young adult when she discovered Champagne was unattainable on the budget of an IHOP waitress and full-time student. Enter cava, prosecco and sparkling wine. These three bubblies are from Spain, Italy and everywhere else, including America, respectively. Unlike Champagne, they are not bound by specific government rules and regulations dating back centuries, so their prices are far lower. For about $10, you can always obtain a lovely sparkler to lend a festive feeling to any occasion—even a simple roast chicken and salad.

Common Novice Cooking Blunders

They all stem from misplaced anxiety. You own the kitchen—make it work for you.

1. **Cooking on low heat.** Don't fear the flame—you can always turn it off.

2. **Not cooking long enough.** It takes a surprising amount of time for a piece of meat to brown well. Don't worry—it probably won't burn.

3. **Cutting things into tiny pieces.** Not only a pain in the ass, but not all that pleasant to eat—big chunks is easier *and* much more interesting.

4. **Using the wrong knife for the job.** People afraid of large knives struggle with tiny ones.

5. **Hovering by the stove.** Force yourself to turn away and work on something else, but keep your ears open for sizzling and your nose trained for new smells.

6. **Not cleaning as you go.** Chaos reigns when your cutting board and your sink get full of crap. Taking a break to tidy up helps clear your mind as well.

7. **Going light on the salt.** If something tastes *enh,* it probably just needs more salt. Even cakes and cookies are better with a touch of salt.

COMMANDO-STYLE ROAST CHICKEN WITH POTATOES

Some people would have you buy a rotisserie chicken from the supermarket and skip all this fuss. Those people are either lazy or scared. Roasting a chicken is easy and takes only as much time as pulling together the rest of the dinner, setting the table and cleaning up your prep dishes. And the only way you can fuck it up is by starting with a chicken that hasn't defrosted properly (and even that's salvageable, by cutting off the legs and letting them roast a bit longer separately).

Just to prove how easy chicken is, we don't even use a roasting pan. "Commando-style" refers to the practice of sticking the chicken directly on the oven rack, a technique first developed by Peter. A tray of thin-sliced potatoes set below the chicken catches the drippings and produces some of the most savory morsels you'll taste. *Serves 2 with leftovers, 3 generously or 4 just fine*

One 4-pound chicken, the localest/organic-est/happiest you can afford

1 lemon

Salt

Assorted fresh herbs, such as thyme, sage, rosemary or oregano (totally optional)

2 cloves garlic

Olive oil

Pepper

2½ pounds russet or Yukon gold potatoes (4 or 5 large)

Preheat the oven to 400°F and place one rack in the middle, with the second rack immediately below it. Unwrap your chicken and dig around inside the cavity and pull out the neck and gizzards, if they're included—sometimes they're in a little paper baggie, sometimes they're just tossed in there, and sometimes you don't get them at all. You just don't want to leave one of the livers in by mistake, as it will flavor the whole bird. (If you like the livers, fry them up as a cook's treat, or just feed them to the cat.) Save the neck to make stock later (see page 63). Set the chicken in a large bowl and pat the skin dry all over with paper towels. To keep the chicken looking tidy, tuck the skinniest part of the wings behind the back (imagine the chicken putting its hands behind its head and saying saucily, "Hiya, sailor!").

Roast chicken over potatoes in oven

Cut the lemon in half, sprinkle it with salt and wedge it inside the chicken cavity. If you have some fresh herbs lying around, you can wedge those in too. Squish the garlic through a press (or chop it very fine), and mix it in a small bowl with a couple of glugs of olive oil, plus a generous amount of salt—about 1 tablespoon—and pepper. Drizzle the garlic-oil mixture all over the chicken—it's messy work, so don't get too anal about it.

Slice your potatoes into ¼-inch-or-thinner rounds and lay them out evenly on a cookie sheet (with a rim!), a large skillet or any other pan that's larger in diameter than the chicken. Sprinkle them with more salt and pepper and slide into the oven on the bottom rack. Slide your greased-up chicken onto the rack above. Wash your hands and your work space thoroughly.

Starting around 45 minutes in, check for doneness: Wiggle a leg to see if it feels loose; when it does, stick a knife into the space between the thigh and the leg, cutting through the skin there and poking the thigh meat. If the juices run pink, give

Raw Chicken = Napalm

Considering our cavalier attitude toward so many other things, you may be surprised to hear us say that raw chicken is very dangerous. But no joke—we cannot stress this enough. We recently watched the DVDs of Julia Child's long-running PBS show, *The French Chef,* and were freaked out to see her blithely touching everything in sight, including her eyeglasses and other food items, with her raw-chicken-juiced-up hands. Whoa, Nellie, how times have changed. Thanks to the rise of nasty-ass factory farms and their highly unsanitary ways, the hygiene buck has been passed on to you, the consumer. Who knows what salmonella lurks in the heart of your chicken? These days it is imperative that you *wash your hands* thoroughly after touching raw chicken and before touching anything else. Every. Single. Time. If you contaminate your kitchen you could be very sorry later, and no one (most of all us!) wants that to happen.

it another 10 minutes; if they're clear, you're done. (If you have a meat thermometer, you're looking for 160°F in the breast and 175°F in the thigh.) If the skin is getting very brown but the legs don't seem close to finished (this can happen if your chicken was cold when you put it in the oven), put some foil over the breast to protect it. How long it ultimately takes depends on the size of the chicken, but 50–60 minutes is usually the window, and remember that the bird will continue to cook a little even once it's out of the oven.

Pull out the bird, place it on a plate and cover it with foil or a big bowl. Crank the oven to 500°F to crisp up the potatoes; you can scatter over some more herbs or very thin slices of lemon at this point, if you like. In about 10 minutes, they should have nice little brown spots on them. When they're done, move them to a platter, leaving behind as much of the chicken fat as you can.

To serve, don't worry about carving off the breasts—just take the whole bird to the table and let people pick at it. But it's a good idea to cut the thighs and drumsticks apart—that is, don't let that whole mass of dark meat wind up on one person's

Invest in Stock

Many people are intimidated by the idea of making their own stock—it seems like a big step into the world of fancy cuisine. In fact, it's a simple process, and little bits of flavorful stock can be used to add richness to vegetable dishes or provide the moisture for braised meats. In bigger quantities, stock gives you a head start on a hearty soup.

The easiest stock starts with your leftover chicken carcass. Put it in a pot with a quartered onion, a carrot (if you have it) and a stick of celery (also optional). Top off with water, add a little salt and bring to a boil. Skim off the scum that comes up during boiling, then turn down to a simmer and leave for about an hour. Pull out the carcass, then pour everything through a strainer, squishing the veg a bit.

Granted, this won't produce the Platonic ideal of chicken stock, but it's a start. To make it better, add the raw neck from the chicken you roasted (you did save the neck, right?). Later, you can graduate to all-raw-chicken stock for more intense flavor. Stash odd chicken bits—more necks, bones, the skinniest bits of the wings—in the freezer until you've amassed a hefty handful, enough for a few cups of stock.

We store stock in a dedicated ice-cube tray (for small doses of flavor) and in quart-size ziplock bags—lay them flat as they freeze, so they're stackable.

plate, because it's probably more than they need or want. In the final picking, don't forget the "oysters," the little nuggets of tender meat that are the chicken equivalent of the tenderloin. They're on each side of the backbone, just above the thighs and below the rib cage—sort of where your own kidneys are.

Note: If you're on top of it, you can brine the chicken to make the breast meat moister and less susceptible to fucking up: Soak it overnight or for at least a couple of hours in 2 quarts water, ½ cup kosher salt and ½ cup sugar. Or buy a kosher chicken, which gets salted beforehand (see page 146 for more details on poultry quality). If you do brine the bird, pat the skin dry thoroughly, or else it won't brown.

GREEN SALAD WITH CURRANTS

The heart of this salad is one that Zora ate during her second year in college, while visiting her not-really-anymore-because-he'd-graduated boyfriend at his friends' Brooklyn apartment for the weekend. Zora felt lucky to be there, among this worldly, citified crew who cooked real dinner for themselves, and this salad, with the clever addition of currants, seemed oh-so-cosmopolitan. Adding crispy croutons and roasting-pan juices came years later—it's a great use of all the chicken goodness. But if you're not roasting a chicken or if you're serving something else starchy, like pasta, skip the croutons entirely—you'll still have a not-so-ordinary salad with a hint of sweetness. *Serves 4*

1 head green leaf or red leaf lettuce

Big handful dried currants (or, in a pinch, small raisins)

1 small red bell pepper

1 shallot or half a small red onion

3 thick slices crusty bread (optional)

Salad dressing (see box, page 65)

Pan juices from roast chicken (optional)

Wash and dry your lettuce and place it in a big bowl—wide and shallow makes the nicest presentation. Scatter the currants over. Slice your red pepper in long, thin pieces—prettier than big square chunks. Slice your shallot or onion into paper-thin slices. Scatter both over the lettuce, then stick the bowl in the fridge. (Lay a couple of damp paper towels over the top if you're doing this more than an hour in advance.)

For the croutons, cut or tear the bread into biggish chunks—about 1 inch on a side is not too big. Toss them into a heavy skillet and slide it into the oven next to the chicken you should have roasting. Pull them out when they get brown and crunchy, about 30 minutes later.

Make your salad dressing (page 65), and when the chicken's done, scrape some of

Never Buy Salad Dressing Again

Nothing kills the "I made this specially for you" feel like plopping a bottle of Wish-Bone on the table. Tamara does have a soft spot for the prefab stuff, and Zora grew up putting ranch dressing on her pepperoni pizza, but on a day-to-day basis, we both prefer a fresh, house-made salad dressing. It's a cinch, and you can keep a batch of it in the fridge for several days' worth of salads.

With a garlic press, squeeze a small or medium-size clove of **garlic** into a jar with a tight-fitting lid—old jelly jars are perfect for this. Add a dollop of **mustard**—Dijon, whole-grain, whatever, but not yellow hot dog stuff. You want, say, ½ teaspoon or so. (Now's about the time to mention that this is not an exact science.) Toss in a pinch of **salt,** and grind in some **black pepper.** Then pour in **vinegar**—we usually use red wine vinegar. For a small batch, you want to pour in enough to reach the level of the first knuckle on your finger. Then pour in double the amount of good **olive oil**—you can eyeball this, because it separates nicely. Put the lid on tight and give a few good shakes, just to the point where you start getting embarrassed about the jiggling in your upper arms. Then open and taste. Frenchie vinaigrette traditionalists usually go with a ratio of three parts olive oil to one part vinegar, but we find that too oily. But you may find our two-to-one ratio too mouth-puckering and extreme, so feel free to adjust. Sometimes, if the vinegar is too tart, just a splash of water will help even things out.

From this basic recipe, there are all kinds of variations: lemon juice or balsamic vinegar instead of part of the red wine vinegar (we never swap out all—lemon is too tart on its own, and balsamic is too sweet), or add a dab of honey, grate in some ginger or mash up an anchovy. For a creamy dressing, mix in a couple of tablespoons of yogurt.

the pan juices (from your tray of potatoes or your roasting pan) into the dressing. (Spoon off a little fat first, if you like, but don't make yourself crazy.) Then shake it all up. Scatter the croutons over the greens. Just as you're sitting down, pour the dressing over the greens. Don't do it any sooner, as the warm chicken juices will make the lettuce wilt, and start light, tasting a lettuce leaf to see if you like the balance. Put any extra dressing on the table, as it's good for the croutons.

BAKED APPLES

These are Zora's go-to post-dinner treat. Serve them as is, or drizzle with a little bit of heavy cream. (If you're feeling fancy, we suppose you could whip that cream, but don't knock yourself out. Ice cream is nice too.) Granny Smiths are the default choice here, as they're reliable year-round. Or experiment with the more interesting varieties that show up in the autumn apple season—but never use Macintosh, because they turn to mush when heated.

Apples

Brown sugar

Ground cinnamon

A lemon or two

Butter

Heavy cream, for garnish (optional)

Preheat the oven to 350°F. Wash your apples (allow one per person, and throw in a couple more for breakfast the next day) and cut out the cores, starting at the stem—a little tedious with a paring knife, but doable, especially when you don't worry about making them look pretty. Be careful not to poke all the way through the bottom of the apple, as you don't want the filling to ooze out. (If you do happen to have an apple corer, take out the entire core, then chop off the end of the core and stick it back in the bottom of the apple, to plug up the hole.) If you think of it, cut a few vertical lines just through the apple skin, to allow it to split as it bakes.

Place the apples in a small baking pan, then fill the cored centers with a big spoonful of brown sugar, packing lightly. Sprinkle with cinnamon. Grate a bit of lemon zest (rind) over each apple, then give a quick squeeze of juice—use only half a lemon for four apples. Dab a bit of butter—less than ¼ tablespoon—on top of each apple, then stick the pan in the oven for 30–40 minutes, until the apples have softened up nicely and your kitchen smells dreamy. Serve whole, or halved if they're small, drizzled with a bit of cream if you like.

CHAPTER 5

SUPER-SECRET CHAPTER FOR VEGETARIANS ONLY!

Brace yourselves, vegetarians—there is a lot of animal flesh coming up later in this book. But although we swagger around with our butcher knives out, it's just for show— our hearts are really with the vegetables. Sure, we plonk down a roast in the middle of the table—because if we didn't, very few men would come to dinner, we learned the hard way. But we really love the variety and color and seasonal surprises you get from greens and grains and cheeses. In fact, Zora was a teenage vegetarian and still thinks in terms of combining proteins. Tamara spent her adolescence working at her parents' fruit stand, learning valuable lessons about melons and spitting cherry pits. As adults we both eat largely—though not dogmatically—veggie most nights of the week. As a result, non-meat-eaters regularly come to Sunday Night Dinner and leave just as stuffed and happy as everyone else.

If you look past the occasional lamb carcass, this book is actually fairly vegetarian-friendly. With just a couple of exceptions, all the side dishes are completely meat-free, and those that aren't are very easily adjusted—look for notes following the recipes for tips on veggie adjustments. To round out all those tasty side dishes, we're including a few purely vegetarian entrées here, along with suggestions for how to fit them in with the menus in the rest of the book. Although we do have to warn you: *Our* vision of vegetarianism, at least, includes a bacon exemption . . . but we'd never force it on you.

FETTUCINE WITH YOGURT AND CARAMELIZED ONIONS (AND BACON?)

This easy and delicious pasta dish is a great recipe for beginner cooks—it's hard to fuck up, and the flavor combination makes it special enough to serve to guests. Zora learned the basic idea from a Greek cookbook by Diane Kochilas, but later adapted it to regular 'Merican ingredients. And, yes, she added bacon—but this pasta tastes pretty delicious without it too. This recipe serves four, because that's about how much you get out of a pound of pasta. If you're doing this for more people, you may want to do the onions in advance, or divide them into a couple of skillets to speed things up.

The only real drawback to this dish is that it's dull and brown—so serve it with a green salad (purslane with olive oil and lemon is very Greek, or go with the Escarole with Roasted Pears and Pomegranate Seeds on page 192), and a simple dessert like the Baked Apples on page 66. *Serves 4*

Olive oil

4 medium yellow or red onions

Salt

8 slices bacon (Totally optional! Really! We're just saying!)

2 cups thick Greek-style yogurt or full-fat yogurt

1 pound fettucine

4 ounces Parmesan, pecorino romano or (more Greek) kefalotyri

Put on a big pot of salted water to boil. Set a cast-iron skillet on the stove on low heat and pour in a couple of glugs of olive oil, then turn to slicing up the onions (use the pole-to-pole technique shown on page 54). Toss the first of your onions into the pan and turn up the heat to medium; once all the onions are in, turn up the heat to medium-high and add salt—say about 1 teaspoon per onion. Stir to distribute the salt, and then don't touch till you hear a bit of sizzling. Turn the heat down to medium and stir periodically while you get the rest of your dinner sorted—the whole caramelizing process will take a good 30 minutes at least. When you turn away from the skillet, keep an ear open for vigorous sizzling—that means the onions need another stir, and maybe another small glug of oil.

If you're opting for bacon, get that going in a separate skillet. Keep the heat low—a not-very-crispy finish fits in best with the other textures in this dish.

Measure out your yogurt into a small bowl. If it's the thick Greek-style, you're set. If it's regular American stuff, beat it up with a fork till it's smooth; if you got the kind with the cream on top (a good idea), be sure to mix that part in.

Get back to your onions. They should have gone from crisp and white to soft and translucent to maybe pale yellow by now. The trick is to keep the heat high enough to turn them overall soft and brown (hence, caramelized), but not so high that individual crispy brown spots form. If it looks like they're getting brown spots, turn down the heat a smidge and add another glug of oil. It's a little depressing to see how much volume they lose as they cook, but that means progress.

When the water's boiling, add the fettucine and cook according to the package instructions, about 10 minutes. During this last stretch, you should have time to finish your side salad; pull out your bacon, drain it and crumble it into biggish pieces; and grate your cheese coarsely.

Before you drain the pasta, take a mug and scoop out some of the hot water. Pour about ¼ cup into the yogurt (a little more if you're using Greek yogurt) and stir to combine—this is to warm it up before it hits the pasta. Then drain the pasta and divide it into four bowls. Top each with yogurt, cheese and onions (and the totally optional bacon, if using). Serve promptly.

SPANISH TORTILLA WITH SAFFRON

This egg dish is the result of two generous gifts. First, Zora learned the technique from a Spaniard, as payback for teaching him the invaluable English idiom *booty call*. Several years later, the second gift appeared: Dapper Dan brought a bag of saffron to dinner—not a wee baggie, but a bag the size of two fists, filled with premium Iranian saffron, acquired via friends of his parents. It felt like the best drug score ever.

Saffron suffers a bit because of its price—"more expensive than gold!" everyone says breathlessly, and then socks a teensy packet of it away on a shelf, to save for some unplanned special occasion (when they'll finally drink that Champagne in the fridge too). We've never subscribed to that school of thought because, really, it's still only a couple of bucks to flavor a whole dish. But with Dapper's saffron gift, we could afford to be even more profligate. We put saffron in everything from lavish lamb stews to humble egg dishes. Hence the saffron-infused tortilla. Yes, it's just eggs and potatoes, in a dish that you could eat at any meal of the day. But add saffron and a generous dose of sweet onions, and it tastes like a splendid treat—even a special-occasion meal.

The truly great thing about a good tortilla is that it can be served at any temperature, and in fact gets better as it sits, as the starch in the potatoes gets all velvety. For this reason, it's great to serve in the summer—you could offer it along with, say, Husk-On Grilled Corn (page 107) and the rest of the Summer in the Yard menu (the grilled tomatoes are especially nice). The eggs also work nicely with the assorted green vegetables in the spring menu, and in winter, it's delicious with the Roasted Grape Tomatoes (page 174) and a Bitter Greens Salad (page 116). If you double the recipe, just use a second pan—a smaller tortilla is much easier to flip. *Serves 4–6*

Large pinch saffron (about 0.4 grams)

Olive oil

2 medium yellow onions

1 pound medium russet or Yukon gold potatoes (about 4)

6 large eggs

Salt

Set a large skillet (10 inches is good) with a lid over medium heat and toast the saffron just until fragrant. Set it aside in a small bowl and crumble it into tiny pieces. Pour a glug of olive oil into the skillet and turn the heat to low, then start slicing up your onions, adding them to the pan as they're ready. When they're all in, add a couple of big pinches of salt and turn the heat up to medium-low. Let the onions soften and turn translucent, stirring occasionally and adjusting if they get too sizzly—this takes about 10 minutes.

While the onions are cooking, scrub your potatoes and peel them (if they're russets) or not (if they're Yukon golds), then slice them up in ¼-inch-or-so slices, then cut those slices in quarters. By now, your onions should be nice and soft. Toss in the potatoes and add another glug of olive oil—you want to make sure the potatoes and onions don't stick at all. Stir and fry the potatoes and onions until everything is well-coated with oil and none of the potato pieces are sticking together, about 5 minutes. Add the saffron, stir well, put the lid on the pan and turn the heat down as low as it will go. If you hear the potatoes start to sizzle more loudly, stir them briefly, maybe add more oil and put the lid back on.

While the potatoes are cooking through, crack the eggs into a small bowl and whisk them up with a fork, just enough to combine the whites and yolks. Add a pinch of salt. After the potatoes have been cooking for 7 or 8 minutes and are tender, take the lid off and scrape them off to one side of the skillet. With your spoon, scrape up any burnt or stuck-on pieces in the pan. Scoot the potatoes to the other side and repeat—you want a nice, smooth, well-oiled surface so the eggs won't stick.

Spread the potatoes and onions evenly out in the pan, turn the heat up to high and pour the eggs in—they should sizzle and set on the bottom—then immediately turn the heat back down to low and put the lid back on the pan. Let the tortilla cook through until the eggs are nearly set, about 8 minutes, but this depends on the size of your pan. There should still be a thin layer of jiggly egg along the top.

Now comes the tricky part: Place a large plate upside-down over the top of the skillet. With your hand on the plate, flip the skillet over to release the tortilla onto the plate. Then slide the tortilla back into the skillet by pulling the plate out from underneath it. Is all of that making you nervous? It should work fine if you've oiled your skillet well, but you can also take the safer route: Turn on your oven broiler and set the skillet under the heat to finish cooking. Keep an eye on it—you want the eggs just to set, but not brown. When it's done, flip the tortilla out onto a plate—or, if the bottom got messed up on the first flip, just slide it out. Cut into wedges to serve. You can eat it hot, but the flavor and texture is even better if you let it cool for about an hour.

TURKISH-STYLE EGGPLANT AND LENTILS WITH GARLIC YOGURT

We know, lentils are a dismal vegetarian cliché. But not **these** lentils. That's because they employ the Best Ingredient Ever: pomegranate molasses (see page 87). The original recipe came from the food saint Musa Dağdeviren, of the Istanbul restaurant Çiya, but we've tinkered with it quite a bit over the years. Dağdeviren roams his country for traditional recipes and rescues them from oblivion. His restaurant is like a culinary museum, and especially great for vegetarians, from the salad greens you never knew existed right on through to the last sip of oregano tea.

This stew is best if you make it one day—or at least a few hours—ahead and then reheat it. Served cold or at room temperature with garlicky yogurt, it's refreshing in the summer; served hot with the optional mushrooms, it's hearty enough to be satisfying in the winter. We'd eat it with the Spring Lamb(less) menu, or with the Fall Means Ham (sans ham) side dishes, and it's great with Rice Pilaf with Cherries and Fennel (page 210), where the garlic yogurt really pulls it all together. Really, we eat it any chance we get. *Serves 8 generously*

For the garlic yogurt:

2 cloves garlic

2 cups thick Greek-style yogurt (see note)

Small handful fresh mint or large pinch dried (see note)

Salt

For the eggplant and lentils:

2 medium eggplants (about 2½ pounds)

Salt

1 cup brown or green lentils

Two 20-ounce packages white button mushrooms (optional)

Olive oil

2 medium onions

6 cloves garlic

2 long semihot green chilies, such as Anaheim or Italian (see note)

1 red bell pepper

4 medium tomatoes, 1 pint grape tomatoes or 2 cups whole canned tomatoes

Big handful fresh mint or 1 tablespoon dried

Red pepper flakes or, better, Aleppo pepper or Turkish-style red pepper (see note)

2 big spoonfuls tomato paste

½ cup pomegranate molasses (see page 87)

Preheat the oven to 300°F. Squeeze the garlic through a press and mix it with the yogurt and mint, plus a large pinch of salt; stash in the fridge till serving time. Cut your eggplants into large cubes (no need to peel). Toss the cubes with a couple of tablespoons of salt and set them in a colander to drain—it helps to set a bowl on top, with some kind of weight (a can of tomatoes, say) in it. Rinse and pick over the lentils, removing anything that even remotely looks like it could be a stone, and put them in a small saucepan with about 1 inch of water to cover. Bring to a boil, then turn down the heat and let the lentils simmer until tender but still holding their shape, about 20 minutes; as soon as they're done, drain the water off.

If you're using mushrooms, clean them and slice them about ¼ inch thick. Set a skillet over high heat and drizzle in a little olive oil; toss in the mushrooms and cook, with a pinch of salt, until nicely browned, about 10 minutes. You should be able to turn your back on them while you prep the rest.

Roughly chop your onions, peeled garlic cloves, green chilies and red pepper and place everything in a large bowl. Chop up your tomatoes and add them too. (If you're using grape tomatoes, cut them in half; if you're using canned ones, crush them in your hand as you add them to the bowl.) Chop up your mint coarsely and toss it in (or sprinkle in dried mint), and add a very small pinch of crushed red pepper—or a large pinch of Aleppo pepper, if you have it. Finally, add the tomato paste and a large pinch of salt and stir to combine.

When your mushrooms are done (if using), stir them in with the lentils. Then pull out a large, heavy pot with a lid. Drizzle a bit of olive oil in the bottom. Empty your eggplant out of the colander and pat it dry with paper towels, squeezing each piece a bit as you go—you want get as much liquid out now as you can, so it doesn't water down the stew. Place about a third of the eggplant in the bottom of the pot, then add about a third of the onion-pepper-tomato mixture, then half of the lentils. Continue layering like this, ending with the onions. Pour additional olive oil—about ⅓ cup—over the top and down the sides of the pot. Drizzle the pomegranate molasses over the top, put the lid on the pot and slide the whole thing into the oven. Bake for 1 hour 15 minutes, until the eggplant is soft. (You can also cook this on the stove top, over very low heat, for the same amount of time.) Refrigerate if you can, to let the flavors meld, then reheat. Just before serving, taste the garlic yogurt again—the flavors will have changed a bit, and it may need a little more salt.

Notes:

- If you can't get Greek-style yogurt, strain 3 cups whole-milk yogurt to thicken it. Line a colander with a clean handkerchief or several layers of cheesecloth and pour the yogurt into it. Gather up the corners of the handkerchief to form a bundle and tie this to your faucet to let the liquid drain off into the sink—1 hour at least, but longer is better.
- Mint is one of the rare herbs that can be really satisfying dried, and it gives the dish an overall earthier flavor that goes nicely with the optional mushrooms. Use it if you can find good-quality stuff at a Middle Eastern grocery.
- The green chilies in this dish are supposed to be mild—the Turkish variety, which are hard to come by, have very little heat. Check your peppers before you add them—if they are notably spicy, just cut down the amount you use.
- Aleppo pepper and Turkish-style red pepper are varieties of mild crushed red pepper, toasted in oil. The pepper gives a rich flavor with only a hint of heat.

BULGUR, CHARD AND FETA–STUFFED VEGETABLES

Karl's father, Steve, is a public defender and a vegetarian, and Tamara's always thinking about new things to feed him that he wouldn't make for himself, especially when his schedule is lighter and he has more time to hang out in the yard. Summer and fall in Tamara's backyard garden (you can take the girl out of Phoenix . . .) is a bounty of gorgeous tomatoes, zucchini and chard, so this recipe almost fell together naturally. Bulgur gives it a nutty flavor, while the spices, pine nuts and feta lend an all-around Mediterranean vibe; basil and lemon zest give it a bright finish. And maybe best of all, it's just as good at room temperature as it is hot. These stuffed veg can happily be combined with the Baked Beets with Balsamic Vinegar (page 130), little wedges of the Spanish Tortilla with Saffron (page 70) and the Green Salad with Currants (page 64) to make a beautiful dinner. *Serves 8*

1 cup toasted pine nuts

4 large ripe tomatoes

4 large zucchini or yellow summer squash

1 medium bunch Swiss chard

7 cloves garlic

1 large yellow onion

Olive oil

½ cup dry white wine

1 cup coarse (#3) bulgur (see note, page 211)

2 cups water

½ cup tomato paste

1 teaspoon ground allspice

2 teaspoons ground sumac (see note)

Handful each fresh parsley and basil

½ pound good-quality feta cheese

1 lemon

Salt and pepper

Preheat the oven to 375°F. Set a skillet over medium-high heat and toss in the pine nuts in a single layer; toast until they turn golden and fragrant, about 5 minutes. Remove from the pan and set aside. Cut the tops off the tomatoes and zucchini. Hollow out the vegetables with a paring knife; cut the zucchini in half lengthwise, then scoop out the centers, to make a little squash canoe. For the tomatoes, you'll probably need to scrape the last bit of tomato seeds out with your fingers. Set all of your vegetable innards aside while you salt the insides of your newly hollowed-out veggies. Then chop up all the veg guts coarsely.

Wash the chard well and trim the stem ends a bit. Chop off the stems and cut them crosswise into small pieces and set aside. Cut the leaves crosswise into long ribbons about 2 inches wide. Peel the garlic and chop it roughly; chop the onion into rough dice. Set a large skillet over high heat and add a few glugs of olive oil. Toss in the onion and garlic and sauté on high for 5 minutes, or until they begin to soften. Add the chard stems and continue sautéing for 5 more minutes. Finally, add the veg innards and a couple of healthy pinches of salt. After another 5 minutes of sautéing, the liquid should have cooked away; at this point, add the white wine, pull the heat back to medium-high, cover the skillet and let everything cook down for about 8 minutes.

Take the lid off the skillet and add the chard leaves. Give the mix a good stir to combine—a pair of tongs is helpful to mix the cooked onions with the uncooked chard leaves. Now pour in the bulgur and mix it in well. Add the water, tomato paste, allspice and sumac. Bring to a boil and let it cook for 3 or 4 minutes, then remove the pan from the heat and put the lid back on. Let it rest for 10 minutes, or until the liquid has been absorbed and the bulgur is tender.

While the bulgur is softening up, chop your parsley and basil, crumble your feta and zest your lemon. Add all of this, plus about two thirds of the pine nuts, to the finished bulgur and taste—add salt and pepper if necessary. If your vegetable shells have released liquid, drain it off. Using a small spoon, stuff the vegetable shells so they're full but not overflowing, then arrange them in a baking pan or on a cookie sheet with a rim. Bake for 30 minutes, or until the shells are cooked through. Sprinkle the remaining pine nuts over the top, along with another good pinch of sumac and/or a squeeze of lemon. Serve hot or at room temperature.

Note: Sumac is a beautiful purple spice with a bright, sour flavor (and is not to be confused with poison sumac—we wouldn't do that to you). Look for it in Middle Eastern groceries. If you can't get it, add an extra squeeze or two of lemon juice.

Date: Monday, February 12, 2007
To: Sunday Night Dinner
Subject: This Sat. 17th! Post VD Bacchanal with
　　My New Cookbook—Au Pied de Cochon

Greetings Hungry Kiddies—

It has been too long.

Karl and I are moved, I am up and running in my new job, Zora is almost finished with her scrivener trauma, Peter is locked in the basement playing Dance Dance Revolution, and Dapper Dan gave me the Most Gorgeous Cookbook Ever for Christmas, so let the games begin! We will be cooking from the ridiculous and fabulous *Au Pied de Cochon* cookbook—complete with cartoons. These people are absolutely out of their fucking minds in the best way; the way I wish more people were. Their religion is foie gras—much and often, and every part of the animal is used. No waste for weak stomachs here! I will be starting out slowly as the recipes are incredibly complicated, so it will either be Lamb Shank Confit or La Coupe PDC (pork loin with béchamel over sauerkraut with mustard sauce), asparagus with sauce gribiche, du Puy lentils, cauliflower/potato purée, and Pets de Soeur to finish it all off (Nun's Farts). Put on your eatin' pants, folks.

In love, garlic and duck fat,
Tamara

PART II

Four Foolproof Menus
(Proofed by Us Fools)

All Sunday Night Dinners
are served family-style.

So now you're armed with some confidence and a stocked kitchen. We're going to walk you through four totally doable weekend meals, one per season. These menus have all been extensively field-tested on hungry Sunday Night Dinner hordes and represent some of the favorite things we've ever cooked, despite their relative simplicity. We're not saying this food is quick to prepare; in fact, you'll want to spend the better part of a day shopping, getting organized and cooking. But we have made sure the recipes here are all but fail-safe, and many recipes allow for some downtime while your oven does the work.

Narrowing the list to just four dinner menus was tough. We've cooked hundreds of big meals for friends since 2003, and each one has been completely different. Going through our old notes, photos and e-mails made us very, very hungry. It also reminded us of all the odd ways we've been inspired: The pope came to visit; it was Columbus Day; it was freakishly warm in January; there was a cold snap in September; Tamara's friend who used to be a vegetarian came to visit; our pal John the Hunter dropped some venison on Tamara's doorstep; we met a carpet salesman in Istanbul who cooked us dinner on his rooftop.

But more often than not, we're simply inspired by really delicious ingredients. We don't get too bent out of shape about local/organic/humane. We buy the best meat that the budget allows, and we can't imagine swearing off saffron, *jamón ibérico* or Indian mangoes just because they come from more than one hundred miles from Queens, New York (especially when everyone else in Queens is enjoying them—and happy to sell them to us). Globalization is just too tasty for us to get righteous about.

But we do get a little obsessed with what's in season. You've likely already learned this lesson the last time you ate a tomato in January—it sucked pink Styrofoam ass, didn't it? Of course it did, because it was grown in a hothouse somewhere at least a six-hour flight away and picked before it was ripe so it would still be "good" while it lounged around in the supermarket for two weeks, waiting for your weak midwinter moment. Humans may be clever (polio vaccines, spaceflight, iPhones, cloning), but somehow still not clever enough to replicate the simple magic that is *in season*. In things like tomatoes, berries, peaches, nectarines, melons of all kinds and even citrus fruits, it makes an enormous difference in taste. We'd think there's some kind of cosmic harmony to the natural goodness of artichokes in March, fall apple cider and bright winter oranges—but then there's the cruel joke that you only ever crave a mojito in summer, forcing your bartender to squeeze juice from off-season stones.

So what to do? Live on potatoes, turnips and cabbage all winter? No, not exactly. Our primary strategy is purely defensive: We just eat the shit out of things when they are in season, to the point where we're almost sick of asparagus/tomatoes/zucchini when the supply starts to dwindle. (We also take the more aggressive move of preserving several quarts of tomatoes at the end of August—very *Little House on the Prairie,* but it takes just a couple of hours, and then we have these little jars of summer to crack open when seasonal affective disorder starts to set in.)

This is all a roundabout way of saying we focused on seasonal ingredients for the following menus. In short, it's the easiest source of inspiration for what to cook, and you get a jump on tastiness when you start with fresh, heavy artichokes, snap beans that really snap, perky greens and sweet, juicy peaches.

But these menus are also merely a suggestion—we hope the flavors and cooking techniques will inspire you to tinker and try new things. Unleash your creativity and take inspiration wherever you find it. The possibilities are truly endless. Let your food guide your occasion or vice versa. The recipes here are meant to be flexible, and we encourage you to make substitutions or otherwise adapt them to your preferences.

The following recipes serve eight comfortably, and we've tried to keep the proportions straightforward, so you can scale up or down with ease.

SPRING LAMB

Practically speaking, little lambs now gambol in the green fields all year round, so the meat itself is no longer a particularly seasonal detail. Not to disrespect the lamb, but, although it goes very nicely with equally tender spring vegetables, it's often just the backdrop. We're basically so desperate for greenery by the time spring rolls around that Sunday Night Dinner menus are always along the lines of "We'll be serving asparagus, and artichokes, and pea tendrils, and fiddlehead ferns, and morels, and ramps, ramps, *ramps!!@!* and . . . oh, yeah, some lamb or something." But it's a good thing we don't serve just the huge vegetable buffet we're craving, because usually the wind gusts cold the night of the dinner, and the big leg of meat is a sturdy, warming thing to cling to.

Unlike our other menus, we don't include a starchy dish, so you may want to serve a good crusty bread alongside—it's especially good for sopping up the lamb juices. Sprinkle the loaf with water, then stick it in a 400°F oven to warm just after you've taken the lamb out.

This menu also requires a bit more than the usual last-minute adjustments, so getting everything finished at the same time can be a little tricky if you're attempting to cook this all by yourself, or if you're working with a limited number of pans. To take some of the pressure off, don't worry about keeping the artichokes warm—they're fine at room temperature. Or use the one-course-at-a-time approach described on page 96. Wrap up the lamb well as soon as it's done, to keep it warm, then serve the artichokes first on their own. Then get up and finish the other two side dishes and carve up the lamb.

SPRING LAMB

- Leg of Lamb with Pomegranate Molasses
- Quick-Braised Romaine with Peas and Mint
- Asparagus and Poached Eggs with Miso Butter
- Plain Old Boiled Artichokes
- Salzburger Nockerl for Beauty School Dropouts

Plan of Attack

1. Measure out Salzburger nockerl ingredients; separate eggs and leave out to come to room temperature. If you're making the optional passion fruit curd, do it now.

2. Prep lamb and stick in oven.

3. Wash and trim lettuce and asparagus.

4. Trim artichokes and set to boil.

5. Make miso butter.

6. Boil asparagus and poach eggs; plate and cover to keep warm if necessary.

7. As soon as lamb is done, cook lettuce and peas.

8. Warm miso butter if necessary and pour over asparagus and eggs; melt butter separately for artichokes.

9. Carve and plate lamb, sit down and dig in.

10. Finish Salzburger nockerl and serve.

Drink Up!

A fuller-bodied red with a little funk to it, such as a Côtes du Rhône, malbec or Rioja, goes well with the lamb (both in the cooking and at the table), but don't spend more than $20 for a good one. Although we always advocate cheap wine, it's especially true here because the only bad thing we have to say about artichokes is that they make wine taste strange and sweet—so you'd be wasting a spendier red.

If you serve the artichokes as a separate course, you could offer a light, dry white—such as pinot gris, muscadet or grüner veltliner, which is also tasty with asparagus. Or (and this is the only time we'll say it) you could just drink water.

Meat Is Murder (Tasty, Tasty Murder!)

News flash: Meat comes from live animals, and very often, *cute* live animals. It's easy to forget this when you're shopping at your local supermarket or Wal-Mart Food Center. Steaks arrive in little foam trays; chicken breasts are conveniently stripped of their bones and skin. We don't like to preach, and you won't see us at a PETA rally anytime soon, but we feel like if you're going to eat meat, you can't be squeamish about it. Get your hands in there—manhandle your roasts, get to know what a whole animal carcass looks like, go to a farm and look a pig in the eye. Respect your meat—and all the ingredients you cook with.

LEG OF LAMB WITH POMEGRANATE MOLASSES

I guess it's not much of a secret ingredient if we jump around cheering, "Pomegranate molasses is the motherfucking best!" One of the best things to come out of the Middle East since algebra, pomegranate molasses is this viscous stuff that hits you all powerful sour but finishes lovable and fruity—it complements rich meats fabulously and (a tip Zora learned on a trip to Syria) can be brushed on fish before you stick it on the grill. We developed this particular lamb treatment quite a few years back, while on a pomegranate molasses bender (yes, it even works in cocktails). The preparation is essentially French—garlic, herbs, anchovies, red wine—but the Syrian Secret gives it a fantastic kick.

And one of the nicest things about using a somewhat exotic ingredient is that it makes something seem fancy when, in fact, all you did was stuff it in a pot and stick it in the oven. (When she's really in a rush, Tamara even skips the stripping-the-herbs step.) The hardest part of the recipe is tying the lamb up—you'll need some kitchen twine, and it helps to have someone to hold the knots. It's also nice to have a meat thermometer (cheap, and usually available even at standard supermarkets), as well as a roasting pan. If a roasting pan sounds like something only grown-ups have, you can also use a big Pyrex casserole dish or something similar—but this is one case where a cast-iron skillet won't do, because the long-simmering wine reacts badly with the metal, making the sauce taste like you just got a cavity filled. *Serves 8*

1 small bunch each fresh rosemary, basil, thyme, oregano and parsley

12–15 cloves garlic

5 anchovy fillets (optional)

1 cup pomegranate molasses

⅔ cup olive oil

2 tablespoons coarsely ground black pepper, plus a bit more to finish

Salt

1 bottle wine, preferably a dry red

One 5- to 6-pound boneless leg of lamb (or 6–7 pounds bone-in)

Preheat the oven to 425°F. Set aside a couple of sprigs of each herb, then strip the leaves off the rest. Peel the garlic and chop it and the herbs roughly—no need to relive that scene in *Goodfellas;* just work it into manageable pieces. Chop the anchovies into small pieces too. Scrape both into a bowl with the herb leaves, then mix in the pomegranate molasses and olive oil. Add the pepper and a bit of salt (a couple of small pinches if you're using anchovies; a couple of larger ones if not), and combine. The mixture should be wet, like a very overdressed salad.

Open the bottle of wine and pour yourself a glass.

Roll out your boneless leg of lamb, pat it dry with paper towels if needed and smear about two thirds of the paste thickly all over the inside. Tamara recommends using your hands, as it's the best way to get in all the crannies—either way, it will be messy, and that's good. Roll the leg up, tucking in the thinner flap of meat at the end, and tie the whole thing up with string. When your blood pressure begins to rise because you cannot get the leg completely closed and your hands are all oily and the twine is slipping, take a deep breath and revisit your wine. Our roasts usually look more like Christmas packages wrapped by a three-year-old who lost his thumbs in a tragic accident than anything a butcher would call his own—we do a few loops around the sides, and then another couple along the length of the roast. Whatever works, you know?

Rub the outside of your tied-up leg with the remaining third of the paste and set the baby, fat side up, directly in your roasting pan or Dutch oven—no need for a rack. (If you're working with a bone-in leg, just slather the meat all over with the paste and drop anything remaining in the pan.) Finish it with a few grinds of pepper. Pour enough of the wine into the pan to come up an inch or so around the lamb, and toss in the herb sprigs you set aside earlier, plus any remaining paste.

Place the lamb in the oven and roast uncovered, checking it periodically. If it looks like it's drying out, add a bit more of the wine or, if you drank all the wine, water. After 45 minutes, poke a meat thermometer deep in the center of the roast (but away from the bone, if your leg still has one). Your goal is 130°F for medium-rare, and keep in mind that the roast will gain a few degrees even after it's pulled out of the oven; also, for the few guests who might want their meat a bit less bloody, there are always the end pieces, which are more cooked through. As soon as your thermometer hits the mark, pull the roast and set it aside, covered, for at least 10 minutes, or as long as it takes to put your side dishes together.

For dramatic presentation, you could bring out the whole hunk of meat—but that creates a 1950s patriarch vibe, as someone has to carve the thing while everyone looks on. We find it easier to slice in the kitchen, arranging the pieces on a platter (rarer to one side, better done to the other) and ladling the pan juices, with the herbs and garlic, over the top. Pass the remaining pan drippings in a separate bowl, as people will almost certainly want a heavier dose of the rich pomegranate magic.

Note: We're lucky to live in perhaps the best neighborhood in the United States for lamb—Astoria's Greek and halal butchers are practically stacked floor to ceiling with gorgeous, tasty little carcasses. But if you can't get a whole leg (or are dealing with a smaller crowd), you can use lamb shoulder chops. Or if a superior pork roast comes easier to you, go ahead and use that—the result is a lot heartier, but also tasty. Beef will even work, though the flavor is just not as distinctly springy.

QUICK-BRAISED ROMAINE WITH PEAS AND MINT

This is a twist on a traditional Roman dish that Tamara discovered while she was doing research on potential Passover foods. Because it was to be both the first Passover she'd ever cooked *and* the first she'd attended, she was desperate for something easy but nonstandard. This tasty combination saved her ass that night, and though she has never been asked to cook the whole meal again, she is always asked to bring this dish. It has also evolved into a (distinctly nonkosher) staple, because the ingredients are usually already hanging around in the fridge and freezer. And even though we swoon over seasonal vegetables, we wholeheartedly endorse frozen peas. Fresh ones require small children to shell them (a natural labor resource we're tempted to acquire), and most of the time they taste like crap anyway because they've turned all starchy while sitting around at the store. So we always have bags of frozen peas in stock—they also come in handy for soothing kitchen bumps and burns. *Serves 8*

1 **large head romaine lettuce**
Handful fresh mint leaves

3 tablespoons butter

One 10-ounce bag frozen peas

¾ cup chicken stock or water

Half a lemon

Wash the lettuce thoroughly, stack up all the leaves and slice them crosswise into 1- or 2-inch strips. Chop your mint fine. In a large sauté pan or skillet, melt the butter over medium heat. Add the peas, straight from the freezer, and cook, stirring occasionally, until they soften and release a bit of liquid, about 2 minutes. Add the romaine and mint, and give a quick toss to coat everything in butter. Pour in the stock, cover for a minute just to steam the lettuce through, then remove the lid and let the liquid cook down for another minute or so more. You want the finished dish to have a tiny bit of broth; the lettuce leaves should be limp, but the stems should still have a little crunch. Just before serving, squeeze the lemon over the dish.

Note: We often make this a summery dish too, adding one or two small zucchini or summer squash, cut into rough cubes, along with the peas, and use basil in addition to or instead of the mint.

ASPARAGUS AND POACHED EGGS WITH MISO BUTTER

High-strung New York City chef David Chang's head would probably explode if he found out how we've disrespected his original recipe for the crazy-savory sauce that tops this dish. The first time we made it, we followed his instructions to the letter, which involved a lot of tender treatment of the butter. The second time we made it, we were frantically behind schedule, and, oops, the butter melted and separated a little. You know what? It still tasted insanely delicious. Since then, we've developed a new technique that doesn't require nearly so much coddling. You can make the mixture a bit ahead and just leave it at the back of or next to the stove—the ambient heat should keep it at the right melting point.

To maximize the presentation of this dish, you need a wide serving platter that has a bit of a lip—this way you can spread out the asparagus and drizzle the miso butter over all of it. And although you will want to drink the miso butter directly from the pan, we have to warn you that doing so *will* make you ill. *Serves 8*

2 bunches asparagus (about 2¼ pounds)

Salt

4 large eggs (see note)

White vinegar, the cheapest you have

Pepper (optional)

For the miso butter:

1 cup dry sherry

4 tablespoons (½ stick) butter, chilled

4 tablespoons miso, preferably white (see note)

Fill a large pot—wider is better than deeper—two-thirds full of water. Add a big, three-finger pinch of salt and put on the heat to boil. Wash and trim your asparagus by snapping off the stem end—they naturally want to break where they become less woody, about an inch from the end. If you're feeling crafty, you can tie the trimmed asparagus in several bundles with twine, the easier to fish the spears out of the water later. Also prep your eggs for poaching: Carefully crack each one into an individual cup, taking care not to gouge the yolks on the shell edges. (If you don't have enough cups, no sweat—just crack all the eggs into a single small bowl.)

For the miso butter, measure the sherry into a nonreactive saucepan, then boil it down to about ⅓ cup—this takes only 5 minutes or so. (If you overboil, just add a bit more sherry and reduce again.) While the sherry is boiling, cut the cold butter into small pieces. Turn off the burner and whisk in the cold butter, 1 tablespoon at a time, alternating with 1 tablespoon of miso. It doesn't look promising at first, but at the end, you'll have a fairly thick sauce that is still pourable. Stow it next to the stove while you finish the asparagus and eggs.

Boil the asparagus for 2 minutes—it should still be nice and crispy and bright green. Remove from the water with tongs and place on a serving plate—it's fine for it to cool a bit. (And if you do lose the thread and get distracted, you can always dunk it back in the boiling water to reheat.) Keep the water boiling—let it heat up again if necessary—and add another big pinch of salt and a couple of big glugs of vinegar. Turn the water down to a medium simmer and gently slide

White miso: We love it 100%.

the eggs out of the cups (or bowl) and into the water, one by one. Let the eggs simmer for 6 minutes, until the whites are set but the yolks still have some jiggle to them. Then carefully remove each one with a slotted spoon, shaking off the excess water, and place directly on the asparagus.

If your miso butter has thickened to the point where you can no longer pour it, set it over a very low flame for about 20 seconds and whisk the bejesus out of it—then pour it over the asparagus and eggs. Sprinkle with a tiny bit of black pepper if you like, poke the egg yolks to make the rich yellow run all over and hustle the platter out to the table.

Sherry, Baby

Although we're much looser in our standards for wine to cook with than most chefs are, we cannot in any way condone the "cooking sherry" sold in grocery stores—it's filled with salt and tastes entirely unlike the real thing. A nice dry *fino* will set you back only about $15, and it lasts forever in the fridge. A delicate *manzanilla* may cost you $20 or more, but it's a lovely complex refresher. Despite sherry's reputation as an old-lady drink (or maybe because of it), we find ourselves nipping at it occasionally before a meal, maybe with some salted almonds. Not a bad investment at all.

Notes:

- Find the freshest eggs possible for this recipe—the whites will hold together better, rather than spinning out like egg-drop soup. If you can't buy from a farmers' market, pick supermarket eggs with the latest sell-by date.
- White miso is preferable to red, both for its less salty flavor and for its light color (the red miso can sometimes look disturbingly like baby poo). Both varieties last just about forever in the refrigerator.

PLAIN OLD BOILED ARTICHOKES

We know there are a million artichoke recipes out there, but we almost never make them. It's not just that we're lazy; it's that we (and when we say *we*, we especially mean Zora) love artichokes so damn much that it seems silly to do anything fancy to them when they taste perfect after just boiling them, and maybe dunking them in butter. (There's a California camp that favors mayonnaise instead. Try them both.) We'll mention a few things you *could* throw in the pot with these guys, but, honestly, that's just to make it look more like a real recipe. Artichokes, water, salt and butter are all you really need.

Although you'll see them in stores most of the year, artichokes have their prime season in spring, and that's when they have the most intense flavor. Pick the heaviest 'chokes you can find (don't worry about a few brownish leaves), and stick to California-grown ones, as those that come from Mexico are usually another variety that gets mushy and tasteless if boiled even a smidge too long. The secret to really intense artichoke flavor is to add tons of salt to the water you're boiling them in. *Serves 8, or 4 major artichoke fans*

⅓ cup salt

4 large artichokes

White wine, we suppose

6 cloves garlic, if you really need to show off

8 tablespoons (1 stick) butter

A few lemons, if you like

Maybe some mayonnaise?

Taming the artichokes

Set a big pot of water on to boil and dump in the salt. Rinse your artichokes and snap off the brown, sad and straggly leaves down at the bottom and along the stem. Slice off just the end of the stem (and just the end, where it looks brownish—that stem is good eatin'). If you're feeling solicitous of your guests' tender fingers, use kitchen shears to snip off the thorny end of each leaf, and slice off the whole top of the artichoke, about half an inch down—but that's all purely cosmetic. More practically, to prevent fights from breaking out at the table, slice each artichoke in half lengthwise. To keep the cut sides from turning brown, smear each side with lemon, or quickly press the halves back together while you're waiting for the water to boil.

Once it's going, dump in the artichokes (and, if you like, the optional wine—a few big glugs will do—and garlic). Cover the pot and let them boil for about 25 minutes. How long they ultimately take to cook depends a lot on their size and freshness—don't be surprised if they take up to 40 minutes. To test, poke the end of a paring knife into the bottom; it should slide in without resistance. When they're done, pull them out and set them in a colander to drain. Then melt the butter and pour it into a few small bowls for dipping (squeeze some lemon in, if you like). If you're going the mayo route, put a few globs into some other small cups, and stir a little so the stuff doesn't look *straight* out of the jar—our California faction likes to add a teeny bit of warm water too, for a saucier consistency.

One Course at a Time

Zora attended a formative dinner party in London in the mid-1990s. It involved wine, candlelight and intellectual debate, and lasted long enough for her to develop a full-blown crush on the hot red-haired guest. What set the tone for this epic evening was the hostess's totally casual attitude, exemplified in her brilliant strategy of getting up to cook the next course only when the guests finished with the last. With such a leisurely meal, the guests never got overstuffed and had plenty of time to chat. Aiming to get everything on the table at once, at the right temperature, is often the most stressful part of cooking a big dinner—but this approach to prep can spare you that. Just have all your veggies washed and other ingredients in order before you sit down. And don't lose track of your duties and drink too much early on. Or do. The party can still turn out just fine—which is another detail to always keep in mind.

Umm . . . then what? you may be thinking. Many times we've dined with folks who've never before tasted the delectable thistle that is the artichoke. Eating them is easier than it looks. Pick each leaf and scrape the soft bottom half off with your teeth—right side up holds more butter; upside-down gives you better traction. When you get into the center, where the leaves are paper-thin, just yank all those off. Then scrape out the fuzzy "choke" with a paring knife or a grapefruit spoon. Dunk the whole delicious heart (and stem) in butter. Then steal your neighbor's, if he's too slow.

SALZBURGER NOCKERL FOR BEAUTY SCHOOL DROPOUTS

You know how when you learn a new word—in English, or in another language—and suddenly you hear it everywhere? It was like that for Zora with Salzburger nockerl. She read about this fluffy-but-simple dessert in *Gourmet,* and the next thing she knew, it was on every restaurant menu she saw, and bloggers were describing heavenly trips to the Alps and the tasty soufflé-ish thing they ate in front of the ski lodge fire. It's a genius concoction that makes it seem like you cared a lot, but really you just whipped up some egg whites and cracked open a jam jar. It should really be called Salzburger knock-'em-dead-erl.

This recipe will serve six people generously and eight more daintily, but after that, you need to double the recipe. And if you do *that,* you need to prep it in two separate batches, as the egg whites will get too big for a standard-size mixing bowl. *Serves 6–8*

5 **large eggs**

¼ **cup heavy cream**

¼ **cup berry or apricot jam, or passion fruit curd (page 99)**

½ **teaspoon salt**

½ **cup granulated sugar**

1 **tablespoon all-purpose flour**

1 **teaspoon vanilla extract**

Confectioners' sugar, for garnish (optional)

Preheat the oven to 400°F. Separate the eggs—this is most easily done when they're still cold, and you simply crack the egg into your hand and let the white run through your fingers directly into a large mixing bowl. (You can also slowly tip the egg between the two shell halves.) Put 3 yolks in a smaller bowl (use the remaining 2 yolks for Passion Fruit Curd, page 99) and set these and the whites aside to come to room temperature. Pour the cream in the bottom of a 9-inch pie plate and tilt to spread it all over the bottom. With a small spoon, dab the jam all over the pie plate too. And resist the temptation to add more than the requisite amount. Contrary to all cooking logic, more jam does not make it better—believe us, we've tried.

In a large bowl, beat the egg whites and salt with a mixer on high speed until foamy. With the mixer running, scatter the sugar slowly over the egg whites. You may get impatient by the end—that's OK, so long as the egg whites are nice and glossy and have stiff peaks when you're done. Turn off the mixer and remove the beaters. Scatter the flour over and fold it in. In a smaller bowl, beat the egg yolks and vanilla together, just until foamy, then fold that quickly into the egg whites too. Don't get too compulsive about mixing it all together, or you'll deflate the whites—it's fine to have some yellow streaky bits.

Now for the fun part: With a big spatula, blob the eggs into the pie plate. Style as desired. Does your Salzburger nockerl rock a Mohawk, perhaps? Or does it have big eighties bangs? Or maybe cute little spikes all over? Stick your coiffed confection in the oven and bake for about 13 minutes, until the egg whites are nicely browned. (If you got a little carried away with the styling, the tips may get quite dark brown. That's fine—someone at the table will like those little burnt-sugar bits.) Be careful not to bang the fluffy thing down on the counter when you pull it from the oven; serve shortly after, with a dusting of confectioners' sugar, if you like.

Passion Fruit Curd

The standard Salzburger nockerl recipe leaves you with a couple of extra egg yolks. Don't let them go to waste. Whip up a batch of this knockout-delicious stuff to dab in the pie plate, along with or instead of your jam; the rest (it makes about 1 cup) you can spread on toast or just eat with a spoon. (Look for passion fruit pulp frozen in flat packs, from brands like Goya—it can also be labeled *maracuya* or *parcha*.) This makes about 1 cup.

¾ cup passion fruit pulp (half a 14-ounce frozen pack)

2 large egg yolks

5 tablespoons granulated sugar

Salt

5 tablespoons butter

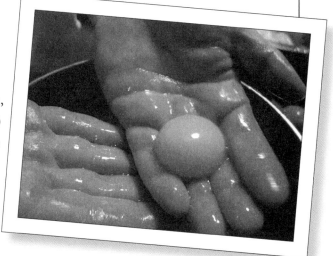

Separating eggs is easier when they're still cold.

In a heavy nonreactive saucepan, melt the passion fruit pulp (if frozen) and boil it down to $1/3$ cup. While it's boiling, whisk the egg yolks with a fork until frothy. When the passion fruit has reduced, stir in the sugar and a pinch of salt, just till dissolved, and turn the heat to low. Spoon a small amount of the hot passion fruit into the egg yolks and stir vigorously. Repeat a few times, until the yolks are somewhat warmed, then pour the whole mixture slowly into the saucepan, stirring constantly. Turn the heat up to medium and continue stirring. As soon as the mixture thickens and starts to hold its shape in the bottom of the pan—only 1 or 2 minutes, though it depends on the weight of your pan—remove from the heat and whisk in the butter, 1 tablespoon at a time. The curd keeps for a couple of weeks in the fridge—as if.

SUMMER IN THE YARD

Is summer really summer without the smell of burning charcoal? Mosquito repellent? Failed deodorant? If it is, we don't know it. Even early on, before we had access to a yard, Sunday Night Dinners moved outside in summer, onto Tamara's small front porch and even onto the sidewalk. We like to think that passersby envied us, but probably they were just annoyed by our raucous laughter and all the wine bottles rolling around. Fortunately no one ever called the fire brigade because our grill wasn't a regulation 10 feet from the house.

We're not suggesting flagrant disregard for fire codes, but we do encourage you to get outside however you can: Finagle your way into renting the neighboring apartment, whose garden you've always admired (that's what Tamara did); make friends with someone with outdoor space; or just take the party to your fire escape or the sidewalk.

Once you're out there, the cooking doesn't need to be all that elaborate. One of our most popular grilled items is Beer Can Chicken—the only labor required is opening the cans beforehand and drinking some of the beer. In the heat, we can't muster much more ambition than to slice up some vegetables—we rely on tasty dressings to deliver flavor, without any slaving over a hot stove. And, really, summer is all about corn and tomatoes—two things that are so tasty on their own, you barely need to do anything to them.

SUMMER IN THE YARD

- Beer Can Chicken
- Dilly Beans
- Butter Lettuce Salad with Yogurt-Mint Dressing
- Husk-On Grilled Corn with Limes
- Grilled Peaches with Duck Fat

Plan of Attack

1. Early in the day, make dilly beans and salad dressing.

2. Read the paper, check out the yard sales, go for a run—whatever.

3. About two hours ahead of dinnertime, prep chicken and set aside to come to room temperature.

4. Wash all vegetables.

5. Light charcoal fire.

6. Drink beer in anticipation of chicken; put chicken on grill; drink more beer.

7. Assemble salad and soak corn in water.

8. Take chicken off the heat; grill corn.

9. Tear those chickens limb from limb.

10. Grill peaches.

11. Don't forget to put out the fire.

The char of the grill typically calls for beer—and you won't go wrong if you just make everyone drink whatever cheap brew you're using for the chicken. Or you could be a smidge classier and offer something with a little more body, such as a wheat beer or a Czech lager.

But wine can also work, particularly a crisp, dry white: Muscadet, sauvignon blanc, pinot grigio, vermentino and vinho verde (the best budget option) are solid choices, as is lesser-known light, dry riesling—look for *kabinett* on the label; those also marked *trocken* are the driest. Sate red drinkers with something not too heavy or mega-fruity, like a pinot noir, gamay, beaujolais (nouveau or otherwise) or Lagrein. Beaujolais in particular takes well to slight chilling—perfect for warm weather.

BEER CAN CHICKEN

Beer Can Chicken is one of those very Southern stunts that you may think requires a friend named Bubba Ed and a bottle of moonshine to pull off, but it's not the case. Tamara did have her first one in Tennessee, but it was made by a Greek man named Kip. She is eternally grateful. The genius of Beer Can Chicken is that you're cooking with two methods at once: grilling *and* steaming. This approach means you get all the flavor of the open flame, while the meat stays moist from the steaming brew. As a bonus, there's lots of cheap beer to drink before you even get the dinner going. *Serves 8*

3 or 4 chickens, depending on your friends' appetites

1 hearty glug olive oil per chicken

Salt and pepper

2 lemons

3 or 4 cans cheap beer, to match your chickens

Worcestershire sauce

About an hour before you want to start cooking and 2 hours before dinner, get your chickens out and love them all up with the olive oil, salt and pepper, giving them a good strong rub inside and out. Then set them aside and let them shake off the fridge chill. While you're in the kitchen, cut your lemons into pieces small enough to get into the pop-tops of the beer cans and set them aside.

Get your charcoal fire going—you want the coals to be medium-hot (so that you can hold your hand about 4 inches over the grill for just 4 seconds), but shoved off to either side, so the chickens won't be sitting directly over the heat. When the coals look ready, call in your volunteers and crack those beers—your guests need to drink about half of each can. (If there's more than half in the can, it will boil over and kill your fire. We mean business—drink up!) Retrieve the half-drunk cans and shake in a few drops of Worcestershire sauce and stuff in a few pieces of lemon.

LEARN FROM OUR MISTAKES!

Sometimes Hot Is a Bad Thing

We know this seems obvious, but please remember that any metal on your grill is *fucking hot all the time.* Also, the beer consumed in preparing a large batch of Beer Can Chicken can make you or your guests a bit unsteady. Bearing this in mind will, we hope, prevent you from suffering the same fate as poor Karl. His very manly yet shapely calf still bears a scar from where he backed into the Beer Can Chicken grill in 2005. And heaven forbid, but if someone does stagger into your grilling station and burn himself, seek medical attention immediately. This isn't the sort of thing you want to let fester.

Less dramatically, and even more obviously, the fire in your grill is also hot. We don't normally believe in super-specialized tools, but for grilling, invest in the longest tongs you can find. Plain old kitchen tongs only result in a lot of red skin and singed arm hair, the smell of which doesn't stimulate the appetite.

Now shove one can up each chicken's ass (we know that's not anatomically accurate, but it's so much more fun to say) and stand the chickens up on the grill, using their legs to form a tripod. Try to leave enough room between them so that you can easily get in with your tongs to maneuver them if need be. Stand back and admire the ridiculous image these chickens create. Put the lid on your grill, being careful not to knock over the chickens, and away you go. Check back in 25 minutes or so and adjust their position if any look like they're cooking unevenly. Depending on their size, they should be finished in 35–45 minutes; a meat thermometer stuck in the chicken thigh should read 170°F, and they should be toasty brown all over.

When you pull them (carefully) off the grill, they should come right off the beer cans. Be very cautious, as those cans will be *hot,* and any remaining liquid in them boiling. Let the chickens rest for 10 minutes or so before digging in, during which time you can throw your corn on the grill.

DILLY BEANS

On the same trip to Tennessee where she learned about Beer Can Chicken, Tamara also insisted on stopping at every single roadside stand—much to her hosts' amusement and, eventually, dismay. Each stand had the same three items: pickled eggs, boiled peanuts and dilly beans. You can call or e-mail us for the other two recipes (some would say they're an acquired taste), but the dilly beans are a must. They will satisfy your palate with the tart pucker of the pickle, and taste like summer with the fresh dill.

You can do this one of two ways. The old-fashioned technique is proper canning, complete with sterilized jars and boiling water. Or you can quick-pickle them the day of your gathering, all in one big bowl. I bet you can guess which method we recommend. Of course you could do this a few days ahead of time, and they'll have even more zing—we just never seem to think of it. You want your beans to be really fresh—they should make an audible snap when you bend them (do this test discreetly in the store). *Serves 8*

1½ pounds green beans

2 big handfuls fresh dill

12–14 cloves garlic

2 cups white or cider vinegar

1⅓ cups water

1½ teaspoons granulated sugar or honey

3 large pinches crushed red pepper flakes (optional)

Salt and pepper

Wash your beans and snap the stem ends off. Put them in a stainless-steel bowl that's deep enough that they can be covered with the pickling liquid. Chop your dill coarsely and toss it on top of the beans. Peel the garlic cloves, crush them and put them in a nonreactive saucepan with the vinegar, water, sugar and crushed red pepper, plus a few generous pinches of salt and freshly ground black pepper. Set on high heat and boil for a couple of minutes. Pour the hot vinegar over the green bean extravaganza, stirring to distribute the garlic and making sure everything's covered. Let the beans sit on your counter until dinner—hours if possible, but at least 30 minutes.

A rare batch of Dilly Beans that made it into a jar

BUTTER LETTUCE SALAD WITH YOGURT-MINT DRESSING

This salad is exceptionally pretty—when we serve it at dinners, we dedicate our biggest platter to it and spread the leaves out flat, the better to scatter the radishes over evenly and make sure there's plenty of dressing on each leaf. Tamara thinks of the yogurt mix as her sophisticate-approved ranch dressing, and it's especially craveworthy in the summertime. It keeps in the fridge for three or four days, so we often make extra just to keep around after the party. *Serves 8*

For the dressing:

¾ cup thick Greek-style yogurt or full-fat yogurt

½ cup buttermilk (optional; see note)

Handful fresh mint leaves

Half a lemon

Salt and pepper

For the salad:

2 heads butter lettuce

2 medium cucumbers

6 radishes

2 scallions

Whisk the yogurt and buttermilk together until well blended. Finely chop the mint and whisk that in too. Cut the lemon in quarters and squeeze it in, one piece at a time, tasting as you go. If the dressing is too thick to pour, you can cut it with a tiny bit of cream or water, but be careful you don't thin it too much. Add salt and pepper to taste and store in the fridge until you're ready to dress the salad.

Wash and dry the lettuce. Keep the leaves whole or tear them up—your choice. Lay them on a salad platter or in a bowl, cover them with a damp paper towel and stick the platter in the fridge while you prepare the other vegetables. Slice your cucumbers and radishes into thin rounds, and chop the scallions—white and green parts—in coarse slices. Scatter these over the top of the lettuce, then grind a little black pepper over everything. Refrigerate again if you need to prepare other things. Just before serving, give your dressing a good mix and check the seasoning again—it may need a little adjustment. Drizzle some over the salad and serve the remaining dressing on the side, in case anyone wants some more. (They will.)

Note: If you don't have buttermilk, just make up the difference with more yogurt. Or do the buttermilk fake-out: Add a healthy spritz of lemon to ½ cup milk, stir gently and let stand 10 minutes. It will thicken slightly.

Juicy Fruit

Lemons (and all other citrus fruits, for that matter) should have a little give to them. If you pick one up and it's rock-hard, think back to the old adage "You can't get blood from a stone" and put it back for some other poor, unsuspecting soul to take home. You only want the softer ones. If you do wind up with some unsuitably firm lemons, roll them on the floor under your bare foot for a minute, to loosen up the oils and juices. (And then, yes, *do* wash them, of course.) As a bonus, your feet will smell great too!

HUSK-ON GRILLED CORN WITH LIMES

Grilling corn in its husk keeps it tender—plus it leaves a fun task for your guests (and less work for you). But husking at the table can be messy—keep trash bags at the ready for the detritus. For eight people, simply soak a dozen or so **ears of corn** in water for about 30 minutes (or, if you forget, at least run the corn under the tap). As soon as you take the chicken off the fire, toss on the corn and leave it, turning occasionally, for 8–10 minutes, or until the husks are browned but not totally charred—meanwhile, the corn has been steaming nicely in its own little wrapper. Serve with butter and wedges of **lime,** plus optional **cayenne pepper.**

GRILLED PEACHES WITH DUCK FAT

One night at the late, great Queen's Hideaway restaurant in Greenpoint, Brooklyn, we got a stunning side dish: peaches poached in duck fat. Brilliant chefs Liza Queen and Millicent Souris had put them on a plate with some slow-cooked pork situation, and we were floored. Later in the summer, we were faced with a dinner where we'd failed to be inspired to make dessert. Then it hit us: peaches *grilled* with duck fat! When dinner is winding down, make your dessert on a warm but not blazing grill. We use peaches most often, but any juicy summer fruit benefits from an encounter with the dying embers. Simply wash, halve and pit some nice ripe **peaches**—one for each guest, plus a few more, as people often behave irrationally around these things. Dip the peach halves in melted **duck fat,** then place gently on the warm grill. Let them mellow for 10–12 minutes, turning once halfway through. They should be soft and a little sizzly. The duck fat is optional, we *suppose,* but damn, it's delicious. If you don't have it (left over from, say, making the cassoulet on page 180, or ordered from a good butcher), butter or walnut oil is a workable substitute, even if neither conjures quite the same decadence.

DOABLE WEEKEND MEAL #3

FALL MEANS HAM

Tamara and Zora moved to New York City around the same time, with about the same amount of money—specifically, none. Though we didn't meet for another four years, it turned out we'd already been on a path to a culinary mind meld, as we'd separately discovered the glory of a cheap ham. Thanks to the ham, perennially available at the supermarket for roughly $1 a pound (in those days), we were able to throw parties for pennies. (What law says you shouldn't throw a party even though you haven't worked in a couple of weeks? If anything, that's when you need the party most!) And a whole ham usually feeds plenty more than eight people, so we were able to send our fellow starving-artist friends home with to-go baggies. The next day, the bone yielded a second hearty dish when boiled with a bag of pinto beans or green split peas. Even though we've finally moved up a bit in the world, we still bust out the ham at least once a year. Proust had his madeleine; we have squishy, pink, water-logged supermarket ham slow-cooked to pork perfection under a cracklike glaze.

We often don't get to the ham until the winter is really upon us, but it's also a great way to sweeten the transition from happy-go-lucky summer to more serious fall. The particular ham treatment we give here started as a staple of our friend Victoria's holiday spread. We tinkered with it a bit, but Zora's mother would still probably disapprove of the glaze (Zora can hear her saying, "It's *pure sugar!*" right now—why does that voice never leave her head?). So that's why we serve it with a good fresh salad of bitter greens, as a little bit of penance. We also sneak turnips into the potatoes, and the fennel, a lovely veg with a soft flavor that's in season throughout the fall, gets some sharp black olives tossed in. Even the dessert is more fruity than sweet, and makes good use of another star of the fall season: apples.

FALL MEANS HAM

- Ham with Bourbon–Brown Sugar Glaze
- More-Delicious-Than-It-Sounds Potato-and-Turnip Casserole
- Roasted Fennel with Black Olives
- Bitter Greens Salad
- Apple Spice Cake

Plan of Attack

1. Prep ham and stick it in the oven.

2. Boil down ingredients for ham glaze.

3. Wash all vegetables, greens and apples.

4. Prep casserole and add it to the oven.

5. Start fennel cooking.

6. Measure out cake ingredients and slice apples (toss with a little lemon juice to keep from turning brown).

7. When ham is nicely browned, pull out and cover. Assemble salad.

8. Remove casserole from oven and let rest. Finish off fennel under broiler if you like.

9. Assemble cake batter, turn down oven and set to bake.

10. Eat dinner.

11. Eat hot cake!

Drink Up!

This is one of those versatile menus that will pair with red or white wine—or even hard cider. Look for French ciders, which are dry and slightly yeasty (in a good way); their crisp apple aroma is perfect with other fall flavors. If you go the wine route, pick a ballsy white, as it needs to stand up to the bourbon in the ham. Rioja blanco (white Rioja), vermentino, white Burgundy, chablis and even the much-maligned California chardonnay all have substance, and if your crowd likes more fruit in a wine, opt for a pinot bianco or even a gewürztraminer. In reds, a lighter, spicier variety will do the trick: a sangiovese from Italy, a carmenère from South America, a tempranillo from Spain or even one of the well-balanced, more subtle cabernet sauvignons from Washington State (those from Napa Valley are often fruitier and higher in alcohol).

HAM WITH BOURBON–BROWN SUGAR GLAZE

Our friend Victoria calls this her Magic Party Ham. She makes it every year for her huge holiday blowout, where we connect with our favorite opera singers, dancers, contractors, headhunters, editors, agents, artists, film preservationists and Victoria's family (both the Sicilian and the Irish sides) from Connecticut. When Victoria cooks, it's never one thing, so the ham shares the table with myriad casseroles, pastas, vegetables, Swedish meatballs. . . . But the ham always emerges the righteous winner. In every other instance, we encourage you to buy excellent-quality meat. But in this case, don't pay more than $1.49 a pound if you can help it, and don't be tempted by the fancy spiral-cut treatment (those thin slices are prone to drying out during the long bake). Yes, we know the evils of megascale pig farming, and we know cheap meat is wrong—but when it's cooked in this bad-ass glaze, it tastes so, so right. *Serves 8–10*

One 10-pound precooked ham, preferably bone-in shank portion

2 cups (about one 500-milliliter bottle) bourbon

2 cups orange juice

3 cups (1 pound) dark brown sugar

5 generous dollops Dijon mustard

½ cup molasses

Salt (optional)

Preheat the oven to 400°F. While the oven is heating, rinse your ham and slice off all the tough outer skin, taking care not to remove too much of the fat along with it—remember, fat is flavor, and by the time this baby is done, the fat will be transformed into tastiness. Then score the shit out of the roast, cutting long crisscrossing lines at least ¼ inch deep and 1 inch apart all over. Sure, it's great to get that pretty traditional diamond pattern, but Victoria says she just "really hacks it up"; the important thing is to make crevices for your gooey, juicy sauce to get in. Place the ham directly in a heavy nonreactive (glass or stainless steel) roasting pan or baking dish and slowly pour ½ cup bourbon over the meat, letting it sink in as much as possible. Set the ham, uncovered, in the oven and let it roast while you prepare the glaze.

In a nonreactive saucepan, boil the orange juice until reduced by half, to 1 cup. While it's boiling, measure out 1½ cups bourbon, plus the brown sugar, mustard and molasses. Off the heat, stir these ingredients into the juice to make a smooth glaze. After the ham has been in the oven for 45 minutes or so, pull it out and apply the glaze all over, making sure you get into all the crevices that have now opened up; pour the remaining glaze into the roasting pan. Return the ham to the oven and let it roast for at least 1½ hours, and up to 2½ hours if you have the time. Check on it every 30 minutes or so, drizzling more of the glaze over the top. Also keep an eye on the glaze on the very top of the ham—this part tends to brown faster, and you may want to wrap it in a bit of aluminum foil (and/or turn the heat down to 350°F) if it looks like it could get burnt before the rest of the ham is properly crisped up.

When the glaze is browned to your satisfaction, remove the glorious ham from the oven, set it on a serving platter and cover it loosely with foil to keep warm. Taste the juices from the roasting pan—you may need to add a pinch of salt to balance it. Pour a bit of this sauce back over the ham, and place the rest in a side bowl to pass with the meat. At the table, designate one guest to hack slices off the ham—it helps keep the crowds from getting unruly.

MORE-DELICIOUS-THAN-IT-SOUNDS POTATO-AND-TURNIP CASSEROLE

We secretly take pleasure in forcing people to eat things they think they won't like, and then having them thank us for changing their minds. That's why we perversely call this a casserole when we could make it sound more appealing by using the fancy French word *gratin*. (Never mind that *casserole* was a French word once too.) And we don't attempt to hide the fact that turnips, the bane of many a Thanksgiving table, are the special ingredient that elevates this from a familiar creamy starch bomb to something rich, intriguing and even a tiny bit spicy. *Serves 8*

6 small or 3 large turnips

4 large russet or Yukon gold potatoes

Big handful fresh thyme sprigs

4 cups heavy cream or half-and-half (see note)

Salt and pepper

2 cups coarsely grated good-quality Parmesan, pecorino romano or even kefalotyri

Preheat the oven to 400°F (see note). Scrub your turnips and potatoes well; peeling them is completely optional. Slice the turnips and potatoes thin, either by hand or in a food processor, and toss them together in a bowl. Pull the thyme leaves from the stems and set aside. Pour a little of the cream into a baking dish (9-by-13 inches, but the larger the better, as it allows for more crusty surface area), just enough to coat the bottom. Arrange some of the turnips and potatoes in a single layer and scatter over some thyme, salt, pepper and a little cheese. Repeat until you get near the top of the dish, holding back some of the cheese for the top. Be sure to leave about ½ inch of clearance, to avoid messy overflow. Pour the cream over the whole thing, then scatter the remaining cheese over the top. Place in the oven and bake for about 1 hour; it's done when the top is attractively browned and you can slide a knife easily through the layers. Let it sit for 10 minutes before serving, to allow the whole thing to set up; it can also sit and wait for quite a bit longer, and be served closer to room temperature.

Notes:

- If you're short on half-and-half, don't substitute a combo of milk and cream—it separates and leaves unattractive lumps all over the potatoes.
- The baking temperature can be dropped to 350°F if you're making this along with something else that requires the lower temperature, but you may want to slide the finished casserole under the broiler for a minute or two just to get the top properly brown and bubbly.

E–Z Clean

Although we don't generally fret over the cleanliness of our ovens (c'mon—they were built to get dirty!), we do occasionally take proactive measures when we're dealing with something that may bubble over and give off smoke. Dishes like fruit pies and casseroles (ahem, *gratins*) are especially prone to this, so we usually slide a cookie sheet underneath the baking pan, or stick a piece of heavy-duty aluminum foil in the bottom of the oven. Whisk it out when you're done (or remove it during the baking, if there's a lot of smoke coming off it), and it's like the boil-over never happened.

ROASTED FENNEL WITH BLACK OLIVES

Because you're eating Victoria's ham, it seems only fitting to serve her dad's Sicilian-style fennel on the side. And because your oven may be too full of ham and turnips, we've adapted his recipe to the stove top. But if you're cooking the fennel on its own, or have a big enough oven, the dish is even simpler—see the note that follows. *Serves 8*

4 large or 6 small fennel bulbs

Olive oil

Salt and pepper

Dry vermouth or white wine

Big handful oil-cured black olives (the wrinkly kind)

Large pinch crushed red pepper flakes (optional, but truly
Sicilian)

Cut the tops off the fennel bulbs—keep some of the fine fronds, but don't be tempted, like we often are, to save any of the pretty green stalks—they're tough and stringy no matter how long you cook them. Then trim off the root ends and cut each bulb into quarters. Set your widest, heaviest (and ideally oven-safe) pan on the stove on medium-high heat and pour in a glug of olive oil. When it's hot, add the fennel and let it brown a bit on every side—don't stir too much. This takes 5–7 minutes when done properly. When the fennel has some good brown spots, sprinkle it with salt and pepper and pour in a couple of glugs of vermouth. Toss in the olives, then cover the pan with a lid or foil and turn the heat down to low. Let it simmer for about 15 minutes, adding a bit more vermouth if the pan gets too dry. When the fennel is easily pierced with a fork but still holds its shape, remove the lid and let any liquid boil away. Sprinkle the fennel with the crushed red pepper. If you want to crisp the fennel up a bit more, slide it under the broiler for a few minutes, until the edges of the fennel are crispy and brown.

Note: To roast the fennel entirely in the oven, simply arrange it in a single layer in a baking pan, scatter the remaining ingredients over it and cover the pan loosely with foil; bake in a 400°F oven for 45 minutes to 1 hour, removing the foil after the first 30 minutes or so to let the fennel brown nicely.

FALL MEANS HAM

BITTER GREENS SALAD

A plain watercress salad sounds boring, but trust us—you'll be better for it. Zora grew up eating a fresh green salad with dinner every single day, a practice she found tedious. As an adult, though, she's still eating her daily lettuce allotment and realizing her parents were right about it keeping her healthy. Meanwhile, Tamara learned the power of salad—particularly digestive-tract-stimulating bitter greens—when she worked at Prune, where one is always on the menu. Tamara became so evangelistic, in fact, that she once advised some customers who'd ordered monkfish liver, bone marrow and sweetbreads (for two!) that they might want some greens "to push it through." She was later chastised for her less-than-appetizing choice of words, but not for the principle itself. It's a solid one that we live by—and it applies especially when you're serving something as hearty and gut-busting as this sweet ham. You can use any or all of the bitter, spicy greens listed, according to what's available. *Serves 8*

2 big bunches arugula, watercress or sweet dandelion greens, or a mixture thereof

Olive oil

1 lemon

Salt and pepper

Give your greens at least three rinses; these all tend to be very sandy, and few things are as unpleasant as grit in your salad. Dry the greens thoroughly, then toss them into a large bowl. Right before you're ready to eat, drizzle a small amount of olive oil over the salad and toss to coat all the leaves. Squeeze on lemon juice to taste (start with half a lemon; you may want a little more) and add a hefty pinch of salt and pepper. Serve quickly; otherwise the greens will start to wilt.

Letting your guests set the table is a good way to keep them out of your hair.

Radishes with butter and salt—
one of our favorite Scooby snacks

Menu for Zora's Indian Vegetarian Extravaganza (art by Karl)

WELCOME TO THE SUNDAY DINNER IN ASTORIA!

FEATURING:

- BOWLS OF DEEZ HOT NUTZ!
- SPICY CUCUMBER SPEARZ! (CHUTNEY'S VEGETARIAN COUSIN)
- PARATHAS WITH COCONUT CILANTRO CHUTNEY,
- CARROT SALAD, USING THE INCORRECT CUISINART ATTACHMENT. AHEM...
- HOMEMADE PANEER WITH PEEEAS,
- CHICKPEAS WITH POTATO & COCONUT,
- LAKE PALACE STYLE EGGPLANT,
- SPICY BUTTERNUT SQUASH, (YUM!)
- WHOLE CAULIFLOWER WITH SPICED TOMATO SAUCE
- DELICIOUS BUTTERY RICE WITH LOTSA PEPPER
- ORANGE BEIGNETS WITH ROSEWATER

KICK OUT YAMS, MO'

MEAT IS MURDER (SWEET, DELICIOUS MURDER.)

Asparagus and Poached Eggs
with Miso Butter (page 91)

Quick-Braised Romaine with
Peas and Mint (page 90)

Baci di Ricotta, post-Peter
(page 130)

Beer Can Chicken (page 102) before,

as the lovely ladies await the heat…

…and after, with a tasty char

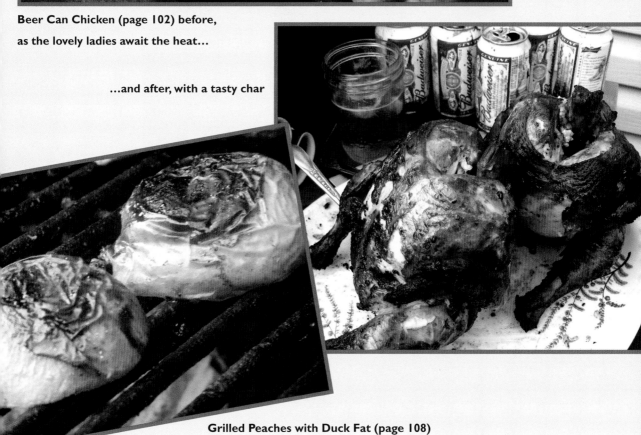

Grilled Peaches with Duck Fat (page 108)

Ham with Bourbon–Brown Sugar Glaze (page 111)

Wax Beans with Arugula (page 170)

The Most Beautiful Sight in the World

Josh's patented fried-chicken technique

Now *that's* what we call summer: Buttermilk Fried Chicken (page 148), Peter's Caesar Salad (page 155), and Sliced Tomatoes with Melted Butter (page 153)

Zucchini and Summer Squash with Brown Butter and Basil (page 128)

Choose-Your-Own-Adventure Cassoulet (page 183): Zora's way…

…and Tamara's way

Oysters (page 165)
right off the grill
(Tamara: "Ooh! Ow!
Hot! Good! Ow!")

Spring 2005:
Tamara and Dapper
shuck oysters for
the waiting crowd.

Zora takes a well-deserved break in her "favorite" apron.

Peter models the Not-So-Whole Roast Lamb (page 206).

Karl shows the Croke (page 217) who's boss.

Less Than Dandy

One day at the bounteous Greek-run produce stand, Tamara was faced with a choice of two kinds of dandelion greens. She chose poorly. But we can't fault her: One kind was labeled SWEET and the other said BITTER. *Sweet*—that must be for wimps, she figured. And besides, the bitter ones were so pretty, all laced with red veins. Turns out, in Greek, *sweet* means bitter, and *bitter* means . . . *really fucking bitter.* Though you may not encounter the Dandy Dilemma in your neighborhood, it's good to know how to handle bitter greens. Some—like arugula, watercress and "sweet" (baby) dandelions—are great for simple salads, dressed just with lemon and olive oil. More intensely bitter greens—such as escarole or chicory—call for something forceful, like a hot bacon dressing, or at least brief cooking (as we do with the Wilted Escarole on page 125). As for true bitter dandelions—apparently only Greek grandmothers can cook those mean little guys as much as they deserve.

APPLE SPICE CAKE

This is a quintessential Sunday Night Dinner dessert, in part because it's something we can throw together at the last second and let bake during dinner (one of our favorite methods, usually starting with the cry, "Shit! *Dessert!*"). More of a quick bread than a cake, it's not the least bit fancy, but its mellow, not-too-sweet familiarity hits the spot after a big meal of more intense and deadly flavors. And it never fails: The morning after we serve this cake, the e-mails start rolling in with requests for the recipe. It has also been used to shamelessly bribe a couple of real estate agents, an eviction-happy landlord, our butcher and the women at the Chanel counter at Macy's, among others. When it's not wrapped up in foil as a gift, we typically serve it with unsweetened cream, whipped up with a shot of brandy. *Serves 8, with extra for breakfast*

Butter, for greasing the pan

3 cups all-purpose flour, plus more for dusting the pan

4 or 5 apples, the crispest variety available (see note)

1 teaspoon baking soda

½ teaspoon salt

1 tablespoon ground cinnamon (see note)

½ teaspoon ground nutmeg

½ teaspoon ground allspice

¼ teaspoon ground ginger

1 cup dark brown sugar

¾ cup granulated sugar

3 large eggs

1½ cups vegetable oil (see note)

¼ cup molasses

2½ tablespoons vanilla extract

1 cup chopped walnuts or pecans (optional)

1 cup heavy cream (optional)

Brandy or cognac (optional)

Preheat the oven to 325°F. Butter and flour a 9-by-13-inch baking pan. Core the apples and chop them roughly. In a small bowl, measure out 3 cups flour and the baking soda, salt, cinnamon, nutmeg, allspice and ginger, then whisk or stir with a fork to combine well. In a large bowl, mash the brown sugar with a fork to get the lumps out, then add the granulated sugar, eggs, oil, molasses and vanilla. Stir well to combine, then stir in the flour mixture, in three batches—don't worry too much about getting an even consistency, as the cake is actually fluffier if the batter is not stirred too aggressively. Add the apples and nuts, if using, and give one final stir to combine. Pour the batter into your pan and bake for 50–60 minutes. Check for doneness with a toothpick or wooden skewer—the cake will be very moist, so don't be afraid if a little bit sticks to the wood. Let it cool on a rack for about 10 minutes. Now's the time to whip up the optional cream with a glug of brandy, if you like. Serve in smallish pieces—ideally you'll have a bit left over for breakfast.

Notes:

- The best apples for this are crisp and a little spicy—we like Cortlands and Braeburns, for instance, but Granny Smiths are always a good fall-back. Avoid the hulking blandness of Golden and Red Delicious apples, as well as Fujis, which have an unappealing thick skin. Deeper in the winter, substitute not-quite-ripe pears for the apples.
- If you have premixed pumpkin pie spice, you can substitute 1 table-spoon of it for all of the spices here, then add 2 teaspoons of cinnamon as well.
- If you bought walnut oil for the Arugula Salad with Oranges and Dates (page 127) and are wondering what else to do with it, use it here instead of the vegetable oil—it lends a lovely light texture and rich taste.

DOABLE WEEKEND MEAL #4

WINTER AND YOUR INNER BRAISE

When winter comes, the nature of Sunday Night Dinner shifts. No more gallivant-ing in the backyard while the sun sets late—or even huddling around the grill for warmth at a last-ditch late-October barbecue. By November, it's back to our roots: all of us crammed around a table in a candlelit room. And whereas in summer we lean on our grill like a culinary crutch, in winter we're addicted to the braise.

We think it's the easiest trick in the book, but braising—slow-cooking in a lower-temperature oven, in a small amount of liquid—never fails to impress. Peter, for instance, still shakes his head in wonder whenever one of us pulls something delicious out of the oven after several hours, as if we'd turned lead into gold before his very eyes. Braising requires several hours, but zero vigilance, and 99.9 percent of the time it turns out an amazingly succulent piece of meat. Tamara takes braising to new lax levels by actually sleeping on the job—as we describe shortly. The results are very rich, so we always go for lighter, acidic side dishes, plus some potatoes to soak up all the delicious juices.

WINTER AND YOUR INNER BRAISE

- Overnight Chuck Roast with Red Wine and Mushrooms
- Wee Salt-Boiled Potatoes
- Wilted Escarole
- Arugula Salad with Oranges and Dates
- Baci di Ricotta

Plan of Attack

1. The day before, shop, then set roast in oven before bedtime.

2. Sleep, and dream of a delicious buffet; wake up and stow the roast in the fridge.

3. About an hour before dinner, set roast in oven to reheat.

4. Wash escarole and arugula.

5. Boil potatoes.

6. Prepare ricotta batter.

7. Slice oranges and prepare salad.

8. Sauté escarole.

9. Sit down to eat.

10. Get up and fry your little ricotta kisses, then keep a sharp eye on your guests' intake.

Drink Up!

Dishes with big, bold flavors can take big, bold wines. Sure, if you love a nice crisp white, then by all means, carry on. But this is a great chance to drink full-bodied reds with a good amount of tannins, or acids. Cabernet sauvignon (from California, Washington, South America or Australia), zinfandel, Bordeaux, syrah (aka shiraz), grenache or a Rhône blend—all of these wines will be fabulous with this menu. But lighter-bodied reds like pinot noir, sangiovese or tempranillo could get a little lost here. Ask your local wine store staff for tips—and if they point you to some funkier Old World wines, take their advice. This food can take it!

The Finishing Touch

Always taste everything you make, every time. It sounds obvious, but it's actually easy to forget this basic step in those last five minutes when you're trying to get everything on the table at once. In any restaurant kitchen worth the price of an entrée, the cooks taste the dishes before they come out. If you discover that your "finished" dish isn't as satisfying as you'd hoped, it may need just a little more salt. If that doesn't work the magic, a splash of something acidic—such as lemon juice or red wine vinegar—can also pull the flavors together. And if (horrors) you discover you've grossly oversalted your food, don't panic. Try adding a little water or white wine and a bit of (unsalted) butter or olive oil, if the dish will support it. If it's a soup or a dish with a bit of sauce, cut up a stray potato and let that boil for a bit, then pull it out before serving; it helps absorb some of the excess salt.

OVERNIGHT CHUCK ROAST WITH RED WINE AND MUSHROOMS

We love braising because you can read the paper while you're doing it. Tamara even gets her beauty rest, putting this roast in right before she hits the sack, then taking it out around dawn, when the smell wakes her up—though it can stay in the oven a good eight hours if need be. The "technique" is simply throwing a bunch of things in a pot and calling it good—we've even shaved off the initial step of browning the meat because it doesn't seem to make much difference in the end. The combo here—rosemary, mushrooms, tomatoes and olives—is a classic one in which the rosemary and olives add a tiny bit of astringency to balance out the fat in the meat. The chilling-and-reheating process only increases the intense flavor. *Serves 8*

One 4- to 5-pound beef chuck roast

1 large yellow onion

15 cloves garlic

Salt and pepper

3 large or 6 small sprigs fresh rosemary

1½ cups oil-cured or Kalamata black olives

One 28-ounce can whole tomatoes

Better part of a bottle of dry red wine

Two 20-ounce packages white button mushrooms

2 tablespoons butter

Preheat the oven to 200°F. Rinse your roast and pat it dry with paper towels. Cut your onion in quarters, then peel your garlic, slicing each clove in half lengthwise.

With a paring knife, poke deep holes all over the roast, inserting half a garlic clove in each one. Generously salt and pepper the whole roast and place it in a heavy Dutch oven or roasting pan with a lid. Nestle any extra garlic, along with the onion, rosemary and olives, around the roast. Drain the tomatoes and add them to the pot, carefully crushing each one in your hand as you go. Pour the wine into the pot, adding enough to come about a third of the way up the side of the roast (how much depends on what size pot you're using). Cover tightly and place in the oven. While you're still up, cut the mushrooms in halves or quarters and sauté them in butter on high heat, until their liquid boils away and they get some nice brown spots. Stash the mushrooms in the fridge.

Go to bed. Dream of tasty meat.

When you wake up, your house will smell absolutely delicious, and your roast will be falling-apart tender. Try to resist eating it for breakfast—instead, stir in the mushrooms, then stick it in the fridge until an hour before dinner. When you take a peek at the chilled stew, you may be a little alarmed by the amount of fat that has congealed on the top. If it's knuckle-deep, you can scrape about half of it off (and freeze it for frying up potatoes some other day). Anything less, don't mess with it—the fat is where the flavor is. Reheat on the stove top or in a 300°F oven for about 45 minutes.

Notes:
- This technique and flavor combo works equally well with both pork and lamb. It can also be prepared with almost any other cheap part of the cow—Tamara's particularly fond of beef cheeks.
- If, for whatever crazy reason, you don't want to do this while you sleep, and you want it done in less than 7 hours, you can turn the heat up to 275°F max (any higher and the meat will not be as tender) and finish it in about 4 hours.

Don't Squeeze, Please

Tamara, already in her clean jammies for the night and in a hurry to hit the hay, learned the hard way that canned tomatoes can be weaponized if handled too aggressively. One quick squeeze, and tomato juice and seeds burst out like projectiles from between the gaps in her not-quite-closed fist. End result: an unplanned wardrobe change right before bed. But if you keep your hand low in the pot, turn the open part of your hand *away* from you and squeeze *gently,* crushing whole canned tomatoes with your hands is in fact faster and tidier than chopping them on a cutting board.

Flavor Sav

Whenever we braise something, we often have pan juices left after all the meat is gone (maybe that's because we can't help but pour in a lot more wine than most recipes call for). Don't toss this delicious stuff—freeze it for flavoring future dishes. You can use it in future meat braises or as the base for a hearty soup. You're really just adding some concentrated wine, herbs and meat juices to your new dish, and that can't hurt at all.

WEE SALT-BOILED POTATOES

This super-simple treatment puts you back in touch with just how innately delicious a good potato is (thank you, Peru!). We always boil more than we think we need, because inevitably someone wanders through the kitchen, tastes one, and then goes on to devour five or six, like they're doughnut holes—and that's not even allowing for the feeding frenzy at the table proper. For eight people, simply fill your biggest pasta pot with water and dump in about a third of a box (no joke—that's an entire pound) of **kosher salt.** Add about 3 pounds scrubbed (but not peeled) **red or yellow small potatoes**—the water should be so salty that they float; if they don't, shake in more salt till they do. Set on high heat to boil for 20–30 minutes, depending on the potatoes' size—they're done when you poke a fork in one and it slides right off without resisting. Drain

Potatoes afloat like people in the Dead Sea.

them and crush lightly with a fork. These are so delicious you could just stop there, without even applying **butter** (and you know they *must* be good if we're saying that!), but if you don't dig austerity, dab on a few knobs, to let it melt in between the crags, and maybe sprinkle over some chopped-up **parsley,** for color.

WILTED ESCAROLE

This is another cheerful advertisement for an excellent "secret" ingredient: anchovies. They add depth to the bitter escarole, making this more than a good-for-you green side dish. If you're not so unethical as to try to feed these to your strict vegetarian guests (*ahem;* see note), then by all means leave them out. But don't skimp on the lemon and crushed red pepper. If you can't find escarole (which looks like butter lettuce with a home perm), chard, chicory or kale works just as well, though let the kale simmer a few minutes longer. *Serves 8*

2 large heads escarole

Olive oil

8 anchovy fillets

Generous pinch crushed red pepper flakes

Half a lemon

Salt (optional)

Wash the escarole thoroughly (dirt loves this green, so be vigilant), then just shake the water off—no need to dry it. Set a skillet on medium-high heat. Add olive oil, then toss in the anchovies. Stir them around until they're nearly melted into goo and very fragrant—this takes a couple of minutes. Crank the heat up to high and toss in your crushed red pepper, followed almost immediately by the escarole (you want the red pepper to heat up in the oil, but not scorch, which can happen in seconds). Stand back as you add the escarole, as the water on the leaves will make the oil pop. It may not all fit in the pot at first; give the greens a quick stir or two, to get everything covered with olive oil and starting to wilt, then add the rest if necessary. Cover the pan and turn the heat down to medium.

After about 3 minutes, remove the lid and turn off the heat. Check for doneness—the stems should be soft, but not mushy. And taste for salt—you may not need any, as the anchovies and their funky brininess will likely have done the work. Spread the greens on a serving plate, squeeze lemon all over and add more crushed red pepper, if you like, and whisk to the table.

Veggie variation: We love anchovies probably a little too much—so much, at least, that we've been known to forget they're an animal product. For a purely vegetarian version of this dish with similar richness, use 1 tablespoon miso in lieu of the little fishes—thin it with a tiny bit of warm water and stir it in just before you take the greens off the heat.

ARUGULA SALAD WITH ORANGES AND DATES

There are two kinds of people in this world: those who can hack fruit in their green salads, and those who can't. And this salad—which is both peppery hot and sweet—may convert the latter camp, simply by confusing them, because the proportions are so skewed in favor of fruit, and there's not a dressing per se, just a mix of oil and orange juice. If you're willing to fork over the cash, walnut oil (in lieu of olive oil) elevates this salad to high art. But check the expiration date when you buy the oil—it's one of those "gourmet" items that languishes on many supermarket shelves. (And if you're not sure what to do with the rest, experiment with it in baked goods, like the Apple Spice Cake on page 117.) *Serves 8*

2 **bunches arugula**

4 **good-quality eating oranges or tangerines**

8 **dates, as large and moist as possible**

Walnut or olive oil

Salt and pepper

Rinse your arugula several times in cold water, dry it thoroughly and place it in a salad bowl. Slice the top and bottom off each orange, then carefully slice the rind off and set it aside. Cut the fruit into thin rounds, removing any large seeds gently with the tip of your knife. Lay the orange rounds on top of the arugula, then scrape any juice on the cutting board into the salad bowl. Squeeze what juice you can out of the orange rind. Pit your dates, slice them into long slivers and scatter them over the oranges. Drizzle a bit of oil over, then sprinkle on salt and pepper. Toss very gently— just enough to distribute a bit of the juice and oil over everything—and serve.

——— Eat Your Vegetables! ———

Although a lot of our menus involve some big ol' hunk of meat, it's often the vegetables we get the most compliments on—even vegetables that many people think they don't like. We feel proud of having converted haters of zucchini, bitter greens, turnips, kale and okra. (We'd claim victory on beets, too, except Tamara *still* hates them—at least she now cooks them frequently because they're in such high demand.) Here are three winning recipes for typically unloved vegetables—we dare your guests not to eat up.

Zucchini and Summer Squash with Brown Butter and Basil

For six or eight servings, slice 4 medium **zucchini** and/or **summer squash** into very thin rounds. (You could also use a mandoline to make long, paper-thin strips—but we're not sure the prettiness is worth the risk of injury.) Finely chop a large handful of **basil** and sprinkle it over the zucchini along with **salt** and **pepper,** and toss to combine. In a small saucepan over medium-high heat, melt 4 tablespoons (½ stick) **butter.** Just after it melts, it will foam up—as the foam begins to subside, the butter will take on a brownish cast, and even begin to smell a bit nutty. As soon as this happens, pull it from the heat and pour it over the zucchini. Toss to distribute the butter, squeeze the juice of half a **lemon** over it and serve before the butter can congeal.

Baked Beets with Balsamic Vinegar

The vinegar helps counteract the dirt-y taste beets can have, and the beet greens give even avowed beet-loathers (like Tamara) a little something to love. For eight or so beet skeptics, snip the green leafy tops from 6 large **beets.** Scrub the beets and place them in a small roasting pan with ½ cup water and several sprigs of **thyme.** Cover tightly with foil and bake in a 400°F oven for 45 minutes. Wash the beet greens and sauté them over medium-high heat with **butter** and a few cloves of crushed **garlic;** after they're wilted, cover the pan and let them simmer (add a little water if necessary) until just soft, about 6 minutes. When the beets are tender, remove them from the oven and set aside until just cool enough to handle. Peel them, cut them into halves or quarters, depending on their size, and toss them in a large bowl with a glug or two of **balsamic vinegar.** Season with **salt** and **pepper** and serve alongside the sautéed beet greens.

Kale with Pickled Red Onions

For most of the late fall and winter, it seems like kale is the only fresh thing to be had. We love this hearty green, but it can get a little monotonous, and it turns a dreary shade of olive when cooked. So we add pickled onions—warmed up with allspice—for exotic flavor, as well as a shot of gorgeous bright pink. For six to eight servings, slice 1 large **red onion** in ¼-inch rings and place in a medium stainless-steel bowl; add two large pinches of **salt** and cover with hot water. Let the onion slices soak while you squeeze the juice from an **orange,** then add enough **red wine vinegar** to make ½ cup, plus another ½ cup water. Bring this to a boil in a nonreactive saucepan with 1 clove **garlic,** 2 **bay leaves** and 5 whole **allspice** berries. Drain the onion slices and pour the boiling vinegar over them; let the mixture sit for at least 30 minutes. Wash and roughly chop two small heads of **kale** (if the stems are large and tough, cut them out). In a large skillet over high heat, briefly sauté the kale in **olive oil** with 4 or 5 crushed cloves of **garlic.** Add about ½ cup **stock** (or water) and simmer, covered, for 8 minutes, or until the stems are tender. Serve topped with pickled onions.

And If None of That Works . . .

. . . apply Candied Bacon (page 134) to the Escarole with Roasted Pears and Pomegranate Seeds (page 192). Candied bacon is a shameless gambit—people would probably eat huge chunks of asphalt if it was served with candied bacon—but it's a fucking delicious gambit. This salad has never failed to stun Sunday Night Dinner guests, who usually demand an immediate repeat at the next party.

BACI DI RICOTTA

Rarely does a recipe come with a warning that also functions as a ringing endorsement. Tamara made these heavenly little fritters called "ricotta kisses" the first time she had a dinner party for Peter and Zora. When Peter laid eyes on the little kisses, golden brown and straight from the fryer, drizzled in honey and set on a platter before him, it was instant *amore*—and he completely forgot the enormous meal he'd already consumed. Eyewitness accounts differ, but he ate at least ten of the *baci*, and possibly as many as thirteen. The next morning, he called Zora, indignant, to see if Tamara had "poisoned anyone else"—he'd been sick in the bushes on his walk home! Zora gently pointed out to him that perhaps he'd done the damage himself—with too many kisses.

Now whenever we serve these, we tell the parable of Peter's Downfall. Do the same, and your guests should be fine. We don't advise anyone eat more than five or six apiece (this recipe makes about fifty). Not only is it easier on the digestion, but also on you, manning the hot oil in the kitchen. If you're leery of deep-frying, don't be. It's surprisingly (dangerously?) simple, and as long as you use a deep pot to control spattering, cleanup is minimal. *Serves 8, with caution*

2 tablespoons granulated sugar

Zest from 1 orange and 1 lemon

1 cup all-purpose flour

3 teaspoons baking powder

½ teaspoon salt

1 teaspoon ground cinnamon

1½ cups (about 1 pound) ricotta (see note)

3 large eggs

1 teaspoon vanilla extract

1–2 tablespoons orange-flower water (optional)

Vegetable oil, for frying (see note)

Confectioners' sugar, honey, or an additional ¼ cup granulated
   sugar, for garnish

Measure the granulated sugar (including additional for garnish, if you like) into the bowl of a food processor, then add the citrus zest; pulse several times to combine and release the citrus oil into the sugar. (No fo-pro? Simply mix the sugar and zest together in a small bowl and set aside.) Measure the flour, baking powder, salt and cinnamon into a small bowl and whisk well with a fork to combine. In a larger mixing bowl, whisk together the ricotta and eggs, beating till smooth; add 2 tablespoons of the citrus sugar, plus the vanilla and the orange-flower water, if using. Then mix in the flour mixture, stirring thoroughly to make a smooth batter. Stash it in the fridge until ready to fry—it can sit for up to a couple of hours.

Pour the oil into a deep, heavy pan (a cast-iron Dutch oven is good)—it needs to be only about 1 inch deep. Turn the burner to high and let the oil get up to about 350°F. (At this temperature, a tiny bit of batter dropped in the oil will bubble furiously and stay on the surface of the oil, not sink.) Using two spoons, drop small dollops of batter into the hot oil. And no matter how much we say *small*, it's nearly inevitable that your first batch of fritters will be a bit too large, and they'll brown before the center is fully cooked. They need to fry until golden brown on the bottom, only about 1 minute, then flip and cook 1 minute more. Lift each one out with a slotted spoon and let it drain on crumpled paper towels while you fry the next batch. Depending on the size of your skillet, you should be able to fry 6–8 at a time, but it's best to maintain a consistent flow of them, to keep the heat steady. When you've fried enough for each guest to have one or two, set them on a plate and dust them with the remaining citrus sugar or confectioners' sugar, or drizzle them with honey—and then send these out to placate the crowd while you finish frying the rest of the batter.

Notes:

- For the most delicate results, it's worth seeking out fresh ricotta from an Italian store or dairy. Supermarket stuff is workable, but you should stir it up separately with a whisk or fork to smooth out some of the graininess.
- You can reuse your frying oil if the temperature never went above 360°F or so, and you strain all the fried bits out. To dispose of frying oil, wait till it has cooled completely, then pour it back into the jug it came in (a funnel is a wise investment). You can then toss it in the trash or gift it to your favorite biodiesel-bus owner.

FOR EXTRA CREDIT:
LANE CAKE, THE GIFT THAT KEEPS ON GIVING

Ninety percent of the time, we serve desserts that are pretty low-key—and that's what we've included in these menus. But occasionally we go a little nuts and invest more time in dessert. If you want to bite off something more challenging for the last course, may we suggest you start with Lane cake? When Tamara read *To Kill a Mockingbird* (not till she was in her midthirties—insert joke about Arizona public schools here), she was particularly interested in Scout's mention of getting "tight" on Lane cake. Any cake that has so much bourbon in the frosting that it's dangerous for a ten-year-old to consume is something she should know about, she reasoned.

Not long after, a friend and fellow waitress named Heather gave Tamara a book that changed her life (no shit): *The Taste of Country Cooking,* by Edna Lewis. Lewis's book is packed with a love of the land and family lore—and a recipe for Lane cake, an old-school Southern layer cake that replaces standard frosting with a rich, eggy and very boozy sauce filled with dried fruits, nuts and coconut.

The first time Tamara made Lane cake coincided with Dapper Dan's first appearance at dinner. Tamara knew Dapper as a regular customer at Prune, Tamara's place of employ—but it seemed like a big social step for him to come to her house. When he arrived, four cake layers and gooey Lane cake topping were strewn around the kitchen, along with the ingredients for other dinner items. We didn't have to worry about any awkwardness: No sooner had Dapper made himself comfortable at the end of the galley kitchen than he'd picked up a big hunk of bacon, which had been waiting to be put in a salad. Then he looked around and spied the Lane cake goo. He promptly dragged the bacon through it and plopped the whole thing in his mouth. "This is really fucking good!" he proclaimed, as he chewed and grinned.

Tamara immediately flew off the handle: "That's my cake frosting, you ass!" she snapped. "And I need that bacon!"

Then she realized: We had a winner. Not just in the frosting-bacon combo, but in Dapper Dan himself. His unmitigated love of food and his willingness to eat anything and talk to anyone has continued to make Sunday Night Dinner a joy. Now we never serve Lane cake without telling this story—and we've even topped off this killer cake with a totally unnecessary garnish of candied bacon, in Dapper's honor.

LANE CAKE, DAPPER-STYLE

One of the many beautiful things about Lane cake is that the bourbon acts as a natural preservative, so the cake can be made a few days ahead of time and left to sit, growing boozier with each passing hour. (In the good old days, Edna says, the cake often sat out for a full week, fermenting in the heat—ah, the Gothic South!) Because we're not native Southerners, though, we've adjusted the topping so it's not quite so deadly sweet, and we've made it a bit runnier, so it's not as thick on the cake as traditional recipes call for. The cake itself is a tasty but resilient one that can withstand a bit of overbaking and other small missteps—we've certainly made them all. Like we need to tell you, but the cake is deadly rich, so a little slice goes a long way—we've made this cake serve at least sixteen people.

For the candied bacon:

½ pound slab or thick-sliced bacon (see note)

1 cup light brown sugar

For the cake:

1 cup (2 sticks) butter, at room temperature, plus more for greasing the pans

3 cups all-purpose flour, or 3½ cups cake flour, if you have it, plus more for dusting the pans

2 cups granulated sugar

Zest from 2 lemons and 1 orange

1 cup milk, at room temperature

7 large egg whites, at room temperature

1 tablespoon vanilla extract

1 tablespoon baking powder

¼ teaspoon salt

For the topping:

1 cup raisins

1 cup bourbon (plus a bit more for the cook)

1 cup chopped dates

1½ cups shredded unsweetened coconut

1½ cups pecans

6 large eggs

7 large egg yolks

1½ cups granulated sugar

1 cup (2 sticks) butter, cut into pieces

2 tablespoons vanilla extract

Measure out the raisins for the topping and combine with ¼ cup bourbon; set aside to soak. While you're at it, pour yourself a little bourbon and add an ice cube.

Make the candied bacon: Trim the rind off the bacon and cut the slab into ¼-inch cubes. (If you're using sliced bacon, just cut the strips into ½-inch pieces.) Put the bacon in a small bowl with the brown sugar, crumbling the sugar to remove any lumps. Toss to evenly coat the bacon with sugar, then lay the bacon out in a single layer, but pressed close together, on a parchment- or wax paper–lined baking sheet with a rim. Scatter the extra sugar over the top. Turn the oven to 400°F and slide the pan into the cold oven. Start checking after 25 minutes or so—the sugar will melt and coat the bacon (don't be alarmed at how it's burning on the pan). At 30 minutes or thereabouts, you should hit the sweet spot of melted sugar and slightly crispy bacon. Remove the bacon from the pan and set on a plate or a paper bag (not on a paper towel). Restrain yourself from eating it immediately—it is dangerously hot. Toss the greasy, sugary parchment paper, and get the baking sheet under some soap and hot water, before any stray bits of sugar harden up.

Make the cake: Preheat the oven to 350°F and butter and flour three 9-inch round cake pans. Place the sugar and citrus zest in the bowl of a food processor and pulse a few times to combine (or simply mix the sugar and zest in a small bowl, to blend in the citrus oil). In a small bowl, combine the milk, egg whites and vanilla, whisking just to combine. In a large mixing bowl, measure out the flour, baking powder and salt; add the sugar. Mix briefly with an electric mixer on low speed, to combine the dry ingredients; then, with the mixer still running, add the butter, about 1 tablespoon at a time. When all the butter is incorporated, the mixture should be dry and crumbly. Then add the milk-and-egg-white mix, in two batches. When it's fairly well blended, crank the mixer up to high and let it run for another 20 seconds or so.

Distribute the batter evenly among the three cake pans—it will be relatively thick, and you'll need to spread it to the edges of the pans with a spatula. Bake for 25–30 minutes, until the top is slightly browned and the cake springs back when touched lightly. Let the layers rest in the pans for 5 minutes or so, then turn them out onto racks to cool completely.

Make the topping: While the cake is cooling, measure out the dates, coconut and pecans; break the pecans into rough chunks. When the cake is cool to the touch, start the topping. In a large nonreactive saucepan over medium heat, stir the eggs, egg yolks, sugar and ¾ cup bourbon together until well blended. Add the butter pieces a couple at a time, stirring constantly. You may need to knock the heat down a notch after a few minutes—you do not want the mixture to bubble or boil, or else the eggs will wind up scrambled. The mixture will start to expand in volume and become a little frothy—you are doing fine. When the mixture has thickened enough to coat the back of a spoon (this may happen before you've added all the butter), remove the pan from the heat; continue whisking in the last of the butter if necessary. Stir in the vanilla, the bourbon-soaked raisins, and the dates, pecans and coconut. The end result should be thick but still pourable. Let it cool just slightly (it will thicken a bit more) as you move on to the next step.

Assemble the cake: Place one layer on a platter and drizzle about 1 cup of the warm topping over it, distributing the fruit and nuts with a spoon. Repeat with the following layers, finally drizzling more topping over the sides and dotting the top with the remaining fruits. You will probably have a bit of the topping left over; if you let it sit and thicken further, you can spread it around the sides of the cake with a spatula, if you like. Finally, scatter the candied bacon over the top of the cake—again, you'll probably have some left over, but that's not a bad thing at all.

Note: For the candied bacon, this is a great opportunity to get a hunk of slab (unsliced) bacon, which is invariably cheaper and better than the standard Oscar Mayer sliced business—but if the latter is all you can get, that's fine too. Incidentally, you can also cook the candied bacon on the stove top—use a heavy skillet, ideally light in color so you can see the color of the sugar. Keep the heat at medium to medium-low—the whole process takes about 20 minutes.

Date: Monday, August 13, 2007
To: Sunday Night Dinner
Subject: Zora's dream of paella in the fire . . . or Sunday Night Dinner . . . this
Sat., Aug. 18!

Hey Hungry Kiddies!

She had a dream . . . a dream of paella in the fire, as in . . . on the grill, baby. Sort of like
the Brünnhilde immolation scene in the Ride of the Valkyries, except with paella.

I am in Sonoma, drinking like it is my JOB. Oh wait . . . it IS my job. At any
rate, I can barely get myself out of the room for classes in viticulture, so I am
using Zora's e-mail to me to describe what will be happening. What I can tell
you is that it will be happening THIS SATURDAY, AUG. 18 at 7 P.M. in the
Reynolds/Wasserman Ranch backyard. Usual rules apply.

Zora: "I think you could just say paella is one of those things they always say is
'a meal in itself,' which means we reserve the right to decide at the very last
second what else we might give you along with clams, mussels, sausages, fish
chunks, chicken bits, saffron, lemons, etc., etc., etc. Oh, and maybe people
should be instructed to bring cheap red wine plus orange or lemon soda to
experience the miracle of 'tinto de verano'—the Spanish technique for
making even the cheapest vino palatable and refreshing.

"Maybe we could have a Syria-style spread of little apps out while we do
the paella—sort of as a nod to the alleged Arabic origins of the word *paella*
(perhaps from *baqiyah,* for 'leftovers'). And by Syria-style, I mean served on
newspaper, and so tasty it will make you weep . . ."

In love and garlic,
Tamara (Mrs.!)

PART III

Get In Over Your Head

Summer 2006:

Katie oversees a deal

id you skip right over the Cautious Beginners section, even though you only cook eggs? Great—you're our kind of people. But even if you did diligently read that first chapter (Zora applauds you, at least), it's really more fun to start here: Think BIG. Or, as Zora's family taught her at an early age: If it's worth doing, it's worth overdoing.

We got in over our heads relatively early in our friendship. We'd been cooking casual meals together—cozy little one-pot braises, freshy-fresh veggies, all relatively normal things— for about eight months, managing to feed our guests well and relatively close to the proper dinner hour. Then the holiday season came around. Chalk it up to too much eggnog or simple insanity, but Tamara rolled out of bed one morning in December and decided she simply *had* to throw a New Year's luau, complete with a whole roast pig—below-freezing temperatures and lack of yard be damned.

Out of sheer ignorance of the folly that lay ahead, Zora agreed. Before she had a chance to process what had happened, she found herself responsible not only for overseeing the pig crackling over the flames, but also for cranking a spit on a roast lamb.

And this is probably the secret of entertaining in a truly grand style: *Jump in blindly.* Don't draw yourself too much of a map or think too hard before committing to a project. If you know from the start how much work the meal will take, and just how much anxiety you'll suffer when things take a turn for the messy (and they always do), then you may be tempted just to go to a restaurant.

But you know what we're going to say: Restaurants are for the weak. Stay home. Work it out. Only a project with a spectacular chance of failure will be a truly smashing success. And if it *does* fail, well, sometimes that's when everyone has the most fun. It promises to be a spectacle either way.

In this section, we'll give you enough information to inspire you. We'll lay out some big ideas—fried chicken, roast oysters, cassoulet, whole roast lamb—and we'll arm you with sufficient detail so you'll feel like you can undertake big projects while keeping a relative grip on the situation. We'll help you banish visions of screaming guests from your head. We'll remind you that when it all seems insurmountable, you should take a moment to sit down, have a drink and collect yourself.

For Sunday Night Dinner, we're used to cooking for twenty regularly. We realize that for most people, that sounds like an overwhelming number. But the great thing about grandiose cooking projects is that they provide some entertainment value of their own. Guests will get as much of a kick out of cranking the lamb spit as they will out of eating the end result, taking a lot of the pressure off you. These are the perfect opportunities to cram your house with guests—and discover that chaos can be fun. Before you know it, you'll be as blasé about twenty hungry people as we are.

 ## Horde Management

Cooking for a crowd can inspire visions of descending locusts, picking their plates clean and then looking desperate for more. We've had the same panic (and done some serious overcatering in our time). Contrary to logic, though, we find it a lot easier to cook a larger number of dishes, rather than enormous quantities of just a few. This way, we don't wind up discovering that our soup pot is too small for the job, for instance. And serving a large variety of dishes creates a feeling of abundance and decadence, even if people don't wind up eating a lot of each thing. It helps, too, that we serve everything family-style—maybe we have better guests than most, but people are pretty good at self-policing portion size when they look down the table to see who else still needs to be fed.

Here's a blanket warning: These meals involve, in various measures, engineering and fabrication, late-night applications of duck fat, boiling oil and fire. They're projects you'd have to be crazy (not) to try. They aren't for the faint of heart, and they do involve taking certain precautions. For us, this has often meant a great deal of Lillet on ice to soothe our frazzled nerves. We of course recommend attempting these dinners, but we also endorse any variation on them you may feel inspired to create—this is only the tip of the iceberg, people.

And oh, yeah—the New Year's luau: *astounding* success. We're not saying it went smoothly by any means, but people still talk about it fondly, years later.

OVER-THE-TOP MENU #1

FRIED CHICKEN FOR A CROWD

You know that recurring dream you've been having for years, where you wake up to the smell of coffee, and some nice older farm lady who has forgotten more about lard than you hope to learn in a lifetime is making a breakfast of fried chicken, biscuits, sausage gravy and sliced ripe tomatoes for breakfast—just for you?

Oh wait—maybe that's *our* dream.

But even if you've never had that dream (now we defy you *not* to have it!), learning to fry your own chicken will change your life, and we're not talking about your cholesterol count. This is about recovering a lost art and making lifelong friends along the way. Because nothing earns positive feedback and sloppy (and maybe a bit greasy) kisses like a hot, succulent thigh encased in a crispy batter—and we don't even mean that in a dirty way.

Not that we were born with this knowledge. We just read the right books, specifically Edna Lewis and Scott Peacock's lovely *The Gift of Southern Cooking*. Edna opened our eyes to the delicate texture that cornstarch adds to the fried coating. Edna whispered, "Make it lard *and* butter in the pan," and coaxed us into frying that piece of country ham first, to flavor the lard and jinx the rule that the first piece of chicken never fries right. Edna tipped us to draining the finished bits of edible gold on more-absorbent crumpled paper towels, not quickly sogged flat ones. With Edna guiding us through, how could we *not* jump up and fry chicken for all our friends and neighbors? Fried chicken—or "yardbird," as our Arkansas-bred friend Grant calls it—has become a Fourth of July tradition, along with a dramatic reading of the Declaration of Independence.

The beauty of fried chicken is that, unlike most other fried foods, you can serve it hot, cold or at room temperature—each has its own charms. So you can work at a leisurely pace and not feel too much pressure. Some overachievers may even be thinking, "Hey, I could fry everything the day before!" Tidy, yes, but that takes away a crucial bit of entertainment from the party—there's something soothing about the lovely sound of sizzling, and the smell is fantastic. And you can even let your guests have a go at the frying—more fun and usually less dangerous than Pin the Tail on the Donkey.

We've intentionally made the rest of the menu uncomplicated—other cold items, and cornbread that's moist enough to make ahead—so once the frying gets underway, you can concentrate on that and dedicate all of your burners to the project if need be. (We've also made it relatively cheap, so you have more cash to throw around on quality chicken—more on that in a sec.) But if you're doing this for only a select crew, instead of the whole neighborhood, then you could stand to be a little more ambitious in the dessert department—the Peach Cobbler on page 175, with its biscuit topping, is a natural accompaniment to the chicken, and it can be made early in the day and set aside.

You may, at this point, be asking nervously, "What do they mean by 'fried chicken for *a crowd*'? How big is *a crowd*?" We'll be straight with you: When we first sketched out this chapter, we called it Fried Chicken for Thirty, because that's what we have done most often. But when we set about testing the recipes for this book and sorting out all the little divergences we'd made from Saint Edna along the way, we got some distance on the whole thing and realized that we may in fact have been totally batshit crazy to fry chicken for the masses. The fact that it takes a long-ass time is just the first of your problems (and we won't tell you the others, because then you'd never do it). But the fact that, on our first try, we managed to shovel fried chicken into thirty gaping maws is testament to the power of not really knowing what you're getting yourself into. Our rationale has always been: If you're going to fry it, why not just fry it for everyone you know?

So, to help you decide how much chicken you should cook, our recipe starts with a flow chart that asks just one simple question (see page 149). All the side dishes make about six servings, geared to accompany the parts from one whole chicken (usually ten pieces, which can serve four or maybe five people)—conservative, yes, but we find it's easier to multiply a recipe (for a longer guest list) than it is to divide.

A note on equipment: You're probably thinking you need a deep fryer to pull this off. It ain't the case, and in fact, you don't want one. We enlisted a FryDaddy-owning friend of Tamara's to take the Cast-Iron Challenge, and he reported (incredulously) that the trusty cast-iron skillet kicked the Daddy's ass. Not only did the chicken fry up more quickly in the cast iron, it also got a brilliantly crisp crust and was just more succulent in every way. The deep-fryer product was soggy and unappetizing. This is one meal for which, truly, no special equipment is needed.

That said, you may need a lot more ordinary equipment than you have on hand. It's more efficient to run the chicken on multiple burners at once. Try to borrow a couple of cast-iron skillets from friends, or branch out and use deeper pots for frying, like Dutch ovens or a Le Creuset casserole (which is just cast iron coated in a fancy enamel anyway)—anything sturdy that can handle the heat. Nonstick pans should be avoided because the metal is usually too lightweight, and the coating is really not meant to withstand steady, high frying temperatures. While you're at it, borrow some baking pans, to put your cooked chicken on when it's finished frying, and some serving platters for the chicken and the sliced tomatoes. Of course, you'll have to invite these pot loaners to dinner once they find out what you're up to, but on the plus side, they'll jump at the chance to lend shit to you the next time.

And no matter how much chicken you're cooking, you'll also need paper towels (a couple of rolls) and tongs. For the buttermilk soak, we use sturdy gallon-size ziplock bags (you can wedge them anywhere in your fridge), but if everything fits in one big pot, and you have room, that'll do just as well. If it makes you feel safer, get a deep-frying thermometer to make sure you're keeping the oil temperatures steady. We have one, but we usually consult it only at the beginning, when we're feeling nervous. Once we're in the swing of things, we forget all about it, and moving the chicken pieces steadily in and out of the fat usually modulates the temperature just fine.

A note on time: You may not need special tools, but you do need to commit some time to frying. Using a single pan, a whole chicken (ten pieces) will take you close to an hour—that's why it's nice to have several skillets going. On the crazy end of the spectrum, eight whole chickens cooked on all four burners could take up to three hours. Which isn't really all that bad, if everyone's chatting and drinking, and you serve some of the chicken pieces early on, to keep the slavering hounds at bay.

A note on chickens: If you're going to all this trouble, you want to start with a great-tasting bird. In an ideal world, you'd go to your butcher, whose name would be Big John (because that's what ours is named), and you'd ask him for the prettiest chickens he has, and he'd deftly cut each one into ten pieces, each breast cut into two pieces crosswise, and the wings with a bit of the breast meat attached so they're not the loser pieces.

But even if the only butcher you know is Sam from *The Brady Bunch,* you still have options. It's of course great to go to your farmers' market and buy organic, free-range, tenderly loved chickens. But we understand if that gets prohibitively expensive for a mob. That leaves whatever's at your local grocery. Only in desperation should you go for the pumped-up bright-yellow offerings from brands that rhyme with Pyson and Turdue. But your grocery store should have its own house-butchered chicken, which will be marginally better, and you get these already cut up. You can then maybe throw in some extra thighs (dark meat is tastier)—go ahead, with our blessing.

There are also some great chickens that have been blessed by people other than us, and they may be available to you too. In New York City, we have the choice of both kosher and halal chickens (the latter can be bought at live-poultry operations, and those fresh-killed lovelies are invariably some lip-smacking good birds). Muslims and Jews will probably get peeved when we say these are roughly the same. But in both cases, religious law is much stricter than the FDA regarding humane treatment before and during slaughter—and that really works in your favor here, resulting in a less stressed, healthier and ultimately tastier chicken. As a bonus, kosher chickens are treated with a brine wash after they're processed, which not only finishes draining out the blood (religious), but also seals in the moisture (delicious). These chickens are very juicy with minimal effort on your part.

So, now that you know how to pick your chick, let's get down to business.

FRIED CHICKEN FOR A CROWD

- Buttermilk Fried Chicken
- Sliced Tomatoes with Melted Butter
- Peter's Caesar Salad
- Guilty-Secret Cornbread
- Melon with Lime and Salt

Plan of Attack

1 day out:

1. Shop.

2. Soak chicken in buttermilk.

3. For overachievers: Make cornbread and croutons.

Show day:

1. Wash lettuce and tomatoes.

2. Make croutons, if you didn't, like us, have Peter make them for you.

3. Make salad dressing.

4. Two hours prior to frying: Take chicken out of fridge.

5. Make cornbread, if you didn't, like us, make it already.

6. Fry, fry, fry and fry some more.

7. Assemble salad.

8. Melt butter for tomatoes.

9. Eat that tasty yardbird!

10. Slice up melon, but wipe grease off fingers before wielding knife.

Drink Up!

What to drink with fried chicken? Beer. In cans. End of story.

OK, OK, you could also go with homemade lemonade, or virtually any white wine—from a crisp albariño (so dry it tastes like licking a hunk of limestone) to a super-aromatic and earthy gewürztraminer (smells like honeysuckle and roses, tastes like melons and, if you're lucky, tart, funky peaches at the end). The most important thing is that you *drink.* Frying is thirsty work.

BUTTERMILK FRIED CHICKEN

We're not giving you exact yields here—only you know your friends' capacity for gluttony. As to how much you feel safe actually cooking, well, we've devised a straightforward flow chart—see opposite.

STEP 1: THE BUTTERMILK SOAK

Regardless of your relative sanity, the prep for one chicken or a million is the same. The night before you're planning to fry, whisk the buttermilk, salt and cayenne together in a stainless-steel or glass bowl big enough to hold your chicken. Drop in your chicken pieces and get your hands in there and make sure everything's coated well.

ARE YOU INSANE?		
NO		**YES**
I'm going to fry a chicken for me and a few friends, and see how it goes.		I want to fry chicken for thirty people. Sounds like fun!
1 whole, in 10 pieces, or a mix of parts	**Chicken**	8 whole, in 10 pieces, or a mix of parts
1 quart	**Buttermilk**	8 quarts
⅓ cup	**Kosher salt***	2 ⅔ cups
1 tablespoon	**Cayenne pepper (optional)**	8 tablespoons
2 cups	**Flour**	Bucketloads
4 tablespoons	**Cornstarch**	Half the box
Some	**Salt and pepper**	A lot
1 quart	**Lard****	6 quarts
1 stick (½ cup)	**Butter**	4 sticks
1 thick slice, about as big as your hand	**Country ham*****	4 thick slices
1 cup, just in case—you probably won't need it	**Vegetable oil**	1–2 quarts

* *If you have only regular table salt, use a bit less, say ¼ cup instead of ⅓ cup.*

** *You want freshly rendered lard, not the deadly hydrogenated 1-pound blocks of it. Go to your Mexican joint and ask for* manteca. *If you can't find it, use vegetable oil.*

*** *We mean that intensely salty Virginia business, ideally. But you could also just use one of those supermarket ham slices—but mind that it will splatter viciously when you drop it in, due to all the moisture.*

This may require more than one bowl—that's fine, as long as it can all fit in your fridge. (And there should be plenty of room, because your tomatoes *do not* belong in there—take them out right now! You are ruining their flavor every second they are chilled like that!) Cover the whole shebang with plastic wrap, or dump the chicken parts and buttermilk into ziplock bags—then stick on a big sign that says RAW CHICKEN, with a skull and crossbones below, close the fridge door and leave it alone for 12 hours to let the salt work into the meat and the milk acids tenderize the chicken.

STEP 2: SETTING UP

A couple of hours before you plan to start frying, take your chicken out of the fridge and set it somewhere out of the way to warm up. Yes, you read that correctly. First we berate you and scare the bejesus out of you about raw chicken, and then we ask you to leave it sitting around to fester—see the following box to see why.

Shake Off the Chill

Particularly for fried chicken, but also for most other meat preparations where timing is crucial, allow the meat to get close to room temperature before cooking. We failed to do this on our second fried-chicken outing. The chicken wound up all beautiful and golden brown, but when our ravenous guests bit into it, they totally freaked. The center, where the meat had been too cold to be affected by the hot oil, was all pink squish. This raw fried chicken has been our only real all-out failure. When the party ends early and you have lots of booze left, you know you've screwed up.

About 20 minutes before you're ready to start cooking, set up your workspace for dredging the chicken. You want an assembly line along the counter, leading toward the stove. Farthest away, start with your big bowl of raw chicken. Next, set up a big plate or two for dredging the chicken. On each plate, combine 2 cups flour and 4 tablespoons cornstarch, plus some salt and freshly ground pepper. (Depending on how much chicken you're frying, you may need to refresh the dredging plates one or more times as you go—just add the same proportions of flour and cornstarch again.) Then, closest to the stove, set a rack on which to rest the dredged chicken pieces (this is optional, but useful if you're going to have three or four pans going).

Also set out a bowl full of warm water, for rinsing the flour-buttermilk goo off your fingers from time to time.

At this point, turn on your oven to 200°F, if you plan to keep batches warm as you go. You should also go close all your closet doors, to keep the fry smell out, and turn on any kitchen fans you may have.

Next, get the fat heating. Set your pans on the stove, and turn on the burners to about medium-high. Pour a quart of lard in each pan, plus a stick of butter. (Now is about the time that we should mention that we don't eat fried chicken every week—this is a twice-a-year-max thing, and even once you realize how it's actually not so hard to fry up a few pieces at a time, you should not start considering this a weeknight meal.)

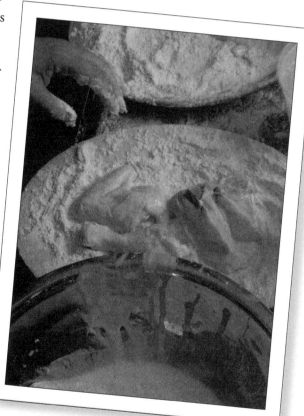

While the fat is heating, set out a big baking pan/tray/what-have-you and cover it with crumpled paper towels—a great job for small children, or your

Dredging the chicken for frying

FRIED CHICKEN FOR A CROWD

obsessive friends who like to do repetitive things. Then turn back to your dredging area and get a few pieces of chicken ready. Start with less-desirable pieces, like wings and backs—think of your first batch as a trial run. Pull each piece out of the buttermilk and shake off the excess goo. Flop the chicken down in the dredging mix, then flip it over—make sure you get flour in all the damp spots. Transfer the chicken to the rack, if you're using one. Your fingers will be equally batter-coated—for this reason, it's nice to have one person do the dredging, and another do the frying.

By now, the oil should be fairly hot, and the butter will be bubbling. Use a big spoon to skim off the ~~scum~~ foam (doesn't that sound nicer?). It's the butter solids rising to the surface, and if left to settle back, they will burn and make the fat nasty. When the oil reaches 350°F (for the thermometerless: Drop in a teeny bit of ham—if it sizzles like crazy, the oil is hot enough), ease in your pieces of country ham. If more foam comes up at this point, skim it off as well. Once the ham is crispy—in about 5 minutes—take it out, drain it on your paper towels and set it aside as a restorative snack for halfway through the chicken frying.

STEP 3: FRYING

Now slip your prepared chicken pieces into the pan, being careful not to splatter the oil everywhere—there will be some popping, thanks to the moisture of the buttermilk. Unless you're using an especially huge pan, three pieces is probably the most you want in there together. If the skillet is too crowded, the temperature will drop, and the chicken will get soggy. Each piece should fry for 6–8 minutes per side. If it seems like it's browning too fast, turn down the heat a smidge—this is all part of the trial run. Resist the urge to flip and fiddle—frying is sometimes a disappointingly passive activity. (Dredge some more chicken pieces to distract yourself.) After the chicken has been going on the second side for 5 minutes or so, you'll notice that the bubbles diminish—this is a sign the chicken is all but done, as a lot of the surface moisture has finally cooked away. To be properly cooked through, the chicken will likely be a bit darker than your standard Popeye's product—that's OK. When you can't stand it any longer, remove the pieces to your crumpled paper towels and salt them a little while they're still hot. (Check the first few for doneness—just stab a knife into the thickest part and look. If the meat is the tiniest bit pink, that's fine—it will finish cooking as it sits, especially if you stash it in the oven to keep warm.) Whenever there's a vacancy in a pan, let the oil heat up again for 20 seconds or so, then slide in a fresh piece.

As the pieces cool, you can move them to serving plates or to the oven to keep warm until you're ready to serve. If your oil levels get a little low, just add some more (lard if you have it, but you can segue to vegetable oil if you like) and wait for it to get back up to temperature before resuming. Occasionally, you may also want to spoon out the burnt bits that are collecting on the bottom of the pan.

When everything's done, wipe the grease off your face, pile your serving platters high and head to the table.

STEP 4: CLEANUP

When you're finished frying, turn off the burners and give the oil a few hours to cool. We like to keep coffee cans around specifically for used oil, but you can also funnel it back into the container it came from and dispose of it that way—anything but dumping it down your drain, or into the yard.

SLICED TOMATOES WITH MELTED BUTTER

This dish is so simple and satisfying it will make you wonder where they've been hiding it your whole life. It has all the beauty of a tomato-and-butter sandwich, without the bread. You need really ripe tomatoes; no amount of good butter can help rock-hard ones. And unsalted butter is best here, as you can then sprinkle salt over the top, which will add a small but appreciable texture contrast. Simply cut good juicy **tomatoes**—one per person if small, half of one if they're large—into thickish "hamburger slices," as Mary Ann dubbed them. Arrange them nicely on a platter, overlapping as little as possible. Melt **butter**—a tablespoon or two for each whole tomato—and then pour it, bubbling hot, over the tomato slices. Sprinkle **salt** over the top, and, if you're craving a little green, toss some **fresh basil leaves** over—entirely optional. Serve immediately, so the butter is still melted when the plate hits the table.

LEARN FROM OUR MISTAKES!

The Hour of Self-Loathing

If only "Nineteenth Nervous Breakdown" were just an awesome song by the Rolling Stones. Alas, all too often, it's our goddamn life. There's nothing like that sinking feeling you get when you realize you've bitten off way more than you can chew. We've felt it *a lot.* In the afternoon before a dinner party, there's this alarming thing that happens with time. At a reasonable hour, you're unpacking your shopping bags and tidying the kitchen. Next thing you know, the doorbell is ringing, your hands are covered with chicken grease, and the only thing you've actually made is the salad dressing. Thus begins what Tamara has dubbed the Hour of Self-Loathing. That's when everyone gets chased out of the kitchen, the music gets cranked, and you just buckle down and work through the blind panic, resisting the urge to curl up in a fetal ball on the kitchen floor.

We've now managed to shrink the Hour of Self-Loathing to the Half Hour of Self-Loathing and, recently, finally, the Fifteen Minutes of Self-Loathing. We hope you can enjoy a steeper learning curve by immediately employing our two strategies: drinking and list making. Drinking is a no-brainer—we pour ourselves drinks as soon as we feel the slightest twinge of stress, a practice we call "clocking in." (This can backfire, of course, if too liberally applied; also if applied the night *before* the party, leaving you to prep with a stunning hangover.) If you don't drink, well, all you can do is take a moment to think back fondly to the days when you did, and just remember the good parts.

List making: also a no-brainer, but it took Tamara years to come around. Now she finds relief and smug satisfaction in crossing things off a list in a way that any life coach would applaud—though that doesn't mean her list isn't scribbled on the back of an envelope and spotted with bacon grease. A prep list also helps keep booze consumption in check, when you can clearly see there are sixty minutes and seven tasks remaining.

But perhaps the best way of getting through the Hour of Self-Loathing is to remember that even though you can no longer see your guests—because you chased them out of the kitchen—they're still having a great time. And they're probably not even hungry yet (especially if you've served them a Scooby Snack—see page 43).

PETER'S CAESAR SALAD

This is not your generic corporate-catered salad, a vehicle for croutons and cheese. No, sir—Peter is a connoisseur of the Tijuana classic, even if he doesn't stick to the original recipe. As an unapologetic lover of anchovies, he prefers the salt-packed whole fish, which are meatier and fuller-tasting, to the oil-packed fillets. Use them if you can get them (you must fillet them yourself: Rinse off the salt, snap off the tail, and peel the sides from either side of the skeleton, using your fingers or a small knife—it will remind you of dissecting earthworms in biology class), but we recognize the ubiquity of the oil-packed sort. Peter is also fervently pro-Greek, and insists that Greek olive oil is superior, as Italian is "too perfume-y"; we like spicier Lebanese and Spanish oils too. Peter's also in the habit of using mayonnaise because we don't always have good, reliable farm-raised eggs hanging around—but if you do, feel free to sub in a raw egg yolk. Not that it changes the flavor much—it just makes you a *chingón* (Mexican for "bad-ass"). *Serves 4 generously, or up to 8 with other side dishes*

1 head romaine lettuce

¼ cup Parmesan, pecorino romano or (if you want to make the Greeks happy) kefalotyri

4 anchovy fillets or 2 salt-packed anchovies

2 cloves garlic

3 lemons

½ cup olive oil

Dollop mayonnaise

Salt and pepper

2 big handfuls croutons (recipe follows)

Wash and dry your romaine thoroughly—lettuce needs to be dry in order for the dressing to stick. As you go, tear each leaf into biggish pieces. (Whole leaves, laid out on a platter, look gorgeous, but are very messy to eat—take our word for it.) Stash the lettuce in a bag or bowl in the fridge, with some paper towels on top. Grate your cheese (or cut it into shavings with a vegetable peeler) and set it aside, covered, while you pull together the dressing.

Chop your anchovies into quarters and your garlic cloves in thirds—if you don't, you'll wind up with two intractable garlic nubbins floating in your dressing. Toss these into a blender (you could also use a food processor, or just a mortar and pestle). Squeeze the juice from 1 lemon into the blender, then add the oil and mayonnaise. Add just a pinch of salt, then grind in a healthy dose of black pepper—more than you might typically use. Whiz everything to blend—give it a good 15 or 20 seconds. Taste the mixture by dipping in a lettuce leaf—you may want a teensy bit more lemon or salt. Set the dressing aside, still in the blender.

Just before serving, arrange the lettuce in a bowl and sprinkle on a little salt and black pepper, then most of the grated cheese. Briefly reblend the dressing if it has separated, then pour it over the lettuce. Toss the salad to coat everything. Scatter the croutons on top—you add them last because they'll sink naturally. Dust on the last bit of cheese for presentation and serve, with whatever lemon you have left, sliced into wedges.

CROUTONS

Peter has a lot to say about croutons, and he insisted they get a dedicated recipe. First, it's best to start with somewhat **stale bread**—Zora and Peter keep a little bowl out on the counter for collecting bread ends just for this purpose. But even if your bread is fresh, use it anyway; your croutons will be somewhat soft, but still delicious. Better bread makes better croutons—you want something with a good chew, not too fluffy ("Yuppie sourdough makes excellent croutons," says Peter). And leave the crusts on. Whether you cut or tear, or go for big or small cubes, is up to you.

You have two approaches to the actual baking: low and slow or hot and quick. For low and slow, spread your bread cubes out on a baking tray or in a cast-iron skillet and stick them in the oven at 200°F overnight, or something near that. The end. Easy, but not incredibly delicious on their own.

The quickie approach requires vigilance, but yields a crouton that's tasty enough just for snacking. Crank your oven to 475°F. In a bowl, toss the bread cubes with enough **olive oil** to coat each and every piece—don't be surprised if you wind up adding quite a lot. Add "a fair amount of **salt,** from very little to a lot, depending on your taste," advises Peter; he also advises **garlic powder,** if you have it (good on popcorn, too, he says). Then spread the cubes out in a cast-iron skillet or two. Stick the skillet in the oven, wait about 3 minutes, then toss the cubes around, and keep checking and tossing every minute until the croutons are golden brown, about 10 minutes—exactly how long this takes depends on your pan and your oven, but croutons can go from golden brown to burnt very quickly, so don't get distracted. (And make sure you have plenty of insulation between yourself and the pan handle—it gets wicked hot.) The instant the croutons are looking nicely browned, pull them out and pour them into a new bowl, as you don't want them to continue cooking in the hot skillet. Let the croutons cool completely—out of sight, to keep kitchen spectators from eating them all—before adding them to the salad.

GUILTY-SECRET CORNBREAD

While testing this recipe, Zora caught Tamara trying to sneak fresh corn kernels into the batter. "I feel so guilty!" Tamara wailed. "How can we tell people to eat seasonally, and then serve *this*?" Hence the name (previously, it had been known as Tamara's Ex-Husband's Cornbread Miracle), and if you too feel bad about passing this titillating combo of boxed mix and canned goods off on your guests, then by all means, add the fresh corn (provided it's late summer). But sometimes you just need something that's dead easy. And it can come in handy outside the fried-chicken context, as it adds a delightful frisson of white-trashiness to an otherwise posh menu. *Serves 8*

One 8.5-ounce box Jiffy corn muffin mix

1 large egg

⅓ cup milk, preferably whole

One 14.75-ounce can cream-style corn (about 1½ cups)

1 jalapeño, sliced thin (optional)

2 tablespoons butter

Preheat the oven to 400°F. In a medium bowl, combine the Jiffy mix with the egg, milk and corn and mix well with a whisk or big spoon. If you want to add jalapeño slices, now is the time. The batter will be very wet—embrace it.

Put the butter in a cast-iron skillet, 9-by-9-inch baking pan or 9-inch round cake pan and stick it in the oven for about 5 minutes, until the butter is melted and the pan is good and hot. Pour the batter into the sizzling pan and bake. Check after 20 minutes, but it probably won't be done for another 5 minutes or so. Test for doneness with a knife or toothpick—you want the center to be a little moist, but not gloppy. The edges will be nicely browned, but the top probably will not be. Let it sit for about 10 minutes before serving.

Notes:

- The cornbread can be made the day before and covered tightly in foil, if you think you can keep people from eating it all.
- This recipe, which serves six comfortably, also multiplies very easily—we've quadrupled this amount to please more than twenty people (baked in a 12-by-16-inch roasting pan, for a tad longer). Doing more than that, though, you're better off dividing it into two or three smaller pans, so the center doesn't get too gummy. If you're making large quantities, it can be easier to beat the eggs separately in a small bowl, then mix everything directly in the buttered baking pan (though you lose the super-crisp crust provided by a preheated pan).

Paprika Butter

Still feeling guilty about the insta-cornbread? Give it a gourmet touch with a side of paprika butter. Simply mix 1 tablespoon **smoked Spanish sweet paprika** (not the hot variety) into 4 tablespoons room-temperature **butter.** Spoon it into a small bowl and pass with the cornbread. A dab of this stuff will dress up anything.

MELON WITH LIME AND SALT

Pick a good **melon** or two and slice it into pieces that people can easily eat with their hands (no need to get cutlery involved). Slice up a few **limes** and squeeze them evenly over all of the melon slices, then sprinkle just the tiniest dusting of **salt** over everything. (If you want the full Mexican treatment, sprinkle on some **cayenne pepper** as well—but it's a taste sensation not everyone wants in an end-of-meal treat.) Serve with paper towels for face wiping.

Nice Melons!

No, we're not looking through your window, commenting on your anatomy. We're looking at a pile of cantaloupe, honeydew, Juan Canary, casaba, Santa Claus, crenshaw and galia specimens, and telling you which ones are the good ones. Tamara spent her teen years enslaved at her parents' fruit stand, and here's what she learned (in addition to the child labor laws):

- Don't shake melons. Just as with your own melons, shaking can cause irreparable damage. In the case of the fruit, it loosens the seeds inside, breaks down the flesh and makes it go bad sooner.

- A ripe melon *smells* like a melon: fragrant, sweet and a little heavy, and maybe even like musk (er, sweat—but "muskmelon" sounds so much more appealing than "B.O.-melon"). There should be a little give at both ends, and less give on the sides, but no big soft spots. Sadly, a rock-hard melon that smells like nothing will never ripen on your counter—it will just go bad. And for the love of Christ, *do not* put a melon in your fridge—the cold air stops the little ripening that does happen off the vine and totally dulls the flavor.

- As for watermelon, you're on your own. People thump and shake and employ all manner of folk-wisdom tests, but the watermelon is a mystery. You never know until you get it home and take it for a test drive—sort of like marriage in the olden days.

AN OYSTER ROAST

We both adore oysters, but we don't eat them as much as we'd like, and we've never been to Martha's Vineyard or Cape Cod or any of those places where people eat them like potato chips. As a result, up until a few years ago, Tamara in particular thought of them only as precious "special-occasion" food to be consumed in fancy restaurants—sort of like surf and turf in the seventies.

Thank Christ, then, when Matt and Ted Lee set her straight. She read an article in the *New York Times* Dining section in which they described a Low Country (another place we've never been) oyster roast. In its original form, the event takes place outside around a grill or fire pit. Guests gather around, someone grills the oysters (in their shells, silly!), and they're immediately shucked and consumed with a minimum of fanfare. The process is chummy and social and doesn't call for a proper sit-down table—but it does provide numerous opportunities for guests to get their hands in the actual prep, without stressing you out that they are fucking up your food.

This all got us thinking. The Lee Bros. had cleverly adapted the whole party to work inside a Manhattan apartment, roasting the oysters in the oven. But, hey, we actually had a grill and a tiny deck—no reason not to use it, even if there wasn't a beach in sight. And because clams are a big thing near us in New York, why not do some of them along with the oysters? And while we were at it, couldn't we pull a table up next to the grill, cover it with newspaper, make a little mignonette (that's the Frenchie name for something vinegary to go on top of the oysters) and scatter a few oyster knives and spoons on it for people to feed themselves—and each other?

Not only could we, but we did, and to smashing effect.

The first time we did this dinner, it involved an exciting and slightly seedy trip to the old location of New York's main fish market, set in the bowels of old Manhattan, way downtown on Fulton Street and right on the East River. It acted (and still acts, at a far less glamorous new location in the Bronx) as the clearinghouse for all of the wholesale seafood in the city. Because the Fulton Fish Market was a very old institution, and mostly wholesale, it operated by its own set of rules: Arrive between 2 A.M. and 4 A.M., bring cash and watch where you're going at all times. The burly workers' huge hooks—last seen in common use in *On the Waterfront*—looked like they could do some serious damage if they were employed for any activity other than moving boxes and big slabs of tuna, and it was rumored that there was boozing on the job.

We arrived early, so we went first to have a couple of beers (one for fun, one for courage) in a nearby tavern that dates back to 1762. When the fish market came to life around 2:15 A.M., we raced across the street to get the first pick on the oysters and clams. We couldn't have made a bad choice. We got one bag of 100 bluepoints from Long Island Sound for $50, 100 small West Coast oysters for $40 and 200 littleneck clams from the sound for $30. (For those of you who like to do the math, this wound up feeding 40 people with a good three dozen mixed clams and oysters left over—although, to be honest, we did panic and serve some pulled pork too, just in case.) After a brief detour to admire the gorgeous choreography that is men in full-length rubber aprons who've been filleting fish all night long for years on end, we hauled our catch back to the car and drove home. By 4 A.M., our bounty was safely stowed in the fridge and we were all in bed.

You may not live anywhere near the Fulton Fish Market or its equivalent, but it's well worth seeking out a wholesale connection for your shellfish—ask at your favorite restaurant if you might order through their purveyor, or just look in the Yellow Pages. Not only will your purchase be cheaper overall, but you'll also get product that's at least a couple of days fresher. If you can't finagle that, cozy up to your local fish store—or the folks at the fish counter in your grocery store—and see what magic they can work. Saying you want to purchase several hundred shellfish at a pop can open some surprising doors.

Before you hand over any cold, hard cash, though, ask when the shellfish were harvested—any more than six days before, and you should move on, as the longer the delay, the more lost souls in the bunch. If they're still bagged, they should have a tag with the harvest place and date. If they're loose, ask about the date, and ask to see the tags if you're skeptical—shops are required to keep them on record. Also pick up a few oysters and check to see that the shells are closed tightly. The fresher and better cared-for they are, the tighter the shells will be. And before you bundle your fresh catch into the car or onto the bus, make sure you have appropriate storage ready at home or at a neighbor's. You don't want to get your pretty babies home and realize you have hard choices to make between the Hershey's syrup and your oysters.

Crowds will flock to this meal, and not just because it involves something most people may only dream of doing. It also gives you the opportunity to "give back" to your guests by allowing them to be as involved in the cooking as they want to be. The natural caretakers in the group can commence with the grilling and feeding, while people who are prone to relaxing can lounge around and get hot shellfish tipped into their waiting mouths. (The best example of this symbiosis that we saw at our first oyster roast was our friend Karine shoveling oyster after oyster toward Karl's seventeen-year-old brother. "I thought he might vomit," said Karine, "but he kept asking for more. I think I fed him about a hundred." Ah, youth.) As a host, you may for once find yourself worrying only about refilling the mignonette; everyone will leave feeling satisfied that they got to contribute too.

If there's one thing that large-scale entertaining has taught us, it's that we're all worker bees at heart. Unless people are cooking at home seven nights a week (or are professional cooks), they're most likely dying to get into your kitchen and help you. From chopping vegetables to stirring sauces to washing dishes, people want so much to help out in the kitchen—especially in social situations. Maybe this is because people are so far removed from day-to-day cooking? Or perhaps it comes from a sense of safety in numbers: *We're all in this together,* the thinking goes, *so I won't fuck it up like I might if I were home alone.* Or maybe it's just our subconscious desire to be a part of something larger than ourselves. Whatever it is, people truly want to be involved, and this is the ideal menu to let them.

We love the idea of doing this dinner in September, when the oysters are tasty and the days are still long, and people are more likely to come outside and hang out for the entire afternoon or evening. That's why we've paired the sweet, briny oysters with hearty potato salad, a heap of greens and some fresh grilled tomatoes to make an easy meal. We end with peach cobbler—but you can use other fruits if the peaches are already past their prime. In practice, though, we've always wound up roasting oysters in colder months—if you're doing this, or following the scheme for roasting indoors, we suggest a couple of small changes. The recipes that follow are designed for twenty when served all together, but when you're drafting the invite list, aim for a crowd as large as you think your place can hold, and then add five or ten. Seriously—this will make you a superstar for the rest of your life, and all it requires is a little courage and ingenuity.

AN OYSTER ROAST

- Oysters and Clams on the Grill
- Oyster Toppings for Every Guest
- Wax Beans with Arugula
- Potato Salad with Bacon
- Grilled Tomatoes/Roasted Grape Tomatoes
- Peach Cobbler

Plan of Attack

1. Acquire your oysters.

2. Make potato salad.

3. Make mignonettes.

4. Wash beans and arugula; prep herb dressing.

5. Assemble cobbler and bake.

6. Start fire in grill and set out all your gear.

7. Wash and prep tomatoes; grill (or roast) to finish.

8. Boil wax beans and assemble salad.

9. Start grilling oysters—and start eating.

Drink Up!

Between the heat of the grill and the brine of the shellfish, nothing complements this menu with the zip and verve it deserves like good lighter-bodied beer. Champagne, of course, would probably work just fine too, but we've never managed to serve it for twenty. If you do want to go with wine, a Portuguese "green" wine—better known as vinho verde—is light, the tiniest bit fizzy and super-delicious. It's also even cheaper than beer, offsetting the sizable investment you're making in the shellfish.

OYSTERS AND CLAMS ON THE GRILL

To start, you need a grill. If you don't have a grill, you can either flip right over to page 200, where we tell you how to rig one up, or borrow one from your neighbor—preferably the neighbor you've been meaning to really get to know. Or you can revert to the Lee Bros. plan and just do this in the oven (see the note at the end of the recipe on page 168). See? The first hurdle is easily overcome!

You should also ideally have two tables. One is set next to the grill and covered with newspaper—this is reserved for oyster activity only, with bowls of mignonette, oyster knives, tongs and the like. The other table, set some distance away, will be for the rest of the food, set up buffet-style. The separation minimizes the chance of burns and other random injuries, and keeps people distributed around whatever party space (yard, deck, living room, sidewalk in front of your house) you're using.

To feed twenty people, you also need:

250–300 oysters and/or clams

Bucket with ice, for stashing uncooked shellfish

Trash can, for trash

Long grilling tongs, for keeping arms singe-free

10 or so dish towels, for wiping down tables, mopping
  brows, grabbing hot stuff and holding cooked oysters while
  prying them open

Drinks to take the edge off, for you

From the time you buy your oysters to the time you start prepping them for cooking, keep them refrigerated and covered with wet paper towels or, if you were lucky enough to be given some, the seaweed they were packed in. Remember—these are still living creatures, and they should be alive until the minute they're put on the fire. (Pause for a morbid shudder.) Don't keep them on ice in the fridge—the fresh water will smother them. If the outside temperature is below 60°F, you can put them directly on your lawn, covered with ice. The ice will keep them cold enough, but melt into the grass and keep them from drowning. This isn't ideal, but in a moment of desperation on Election Day 2008, we discovered it can work. Wouldn't it be brilliant if you happened to have a giant saltwater aquarium you could toss them into? You probably don't, but we mention it just in case. . . .

About an hour before you're planning to start the fire, wash your oysters thoroughly and give them a little scrub to remove any obvious dirt/mud/barnacles and so on. But no need to go overboard with this—you're not eating the shells, after all. At this point, you can place them in something large enough to hold them and just a bit of ice so they stay well chilled until they hit the grill.

Get the fire blazing, and set the grill 4–6 inches above the flames. We always take the road that ends in the wood coal fire, but we understand if you love your fancy-pants propane grill—set it just about as high as it will go. When the fire is very hot—when you can hold your hand about 4 inches above the grill for just a couple of seconds—you're ready to start throwing the shellfish on. But before you get cooking, check that everything else is in place: Mignonettes are on the table next to the grill, the side dishes are laid out, all drinks are refreshed. The shellfish take only a few minutes to cook, so you want to devote all your attention to them once the process is in motion.

Ready? Place as many oysters and clams as you can fit on the grill without crowd-ing; you need just enough space between to pick them up easily with tongs. (But once they're on, there's no need to flip them.) You or one of your volunteer grillers should keep close watch: As soon as they pop open, after 6–9 minutes for oysters and 5–8 minutes for clams, they're perfectly cooked and can come right off.

If any shellfish do not pop after 10 minutes, you have a small dilemma. If only one or two oysters in a batch of a dozen don't open, toss them. There will always be a few dead soldiers—the cost of doing business. But if none of your oysters are open-ing, you may have a rare intractable batch—a combination of very sturdy shells and not-so-moist innards that don't produce enough steam pressure. If you *know* they're freshly harvested, and you've cared for them well up until the time they hit the grill, you can probably eat them without harm (we have done so, nervously, but with no ill effect). But if you have even the slightest doubt as to the overall health and liveliness of your oysters, *do not* eat them. It's a sad thing, but ptomaine poisoning is just not something that should be brought about through frugality.

LEARN FROM OUR MISTAKES!

Too Hot to Handle

We sure are! But seriously, so are oyster and clam shells straight off the grill. Like slow-learning rats in a lab, we kept reaching for them all the same—they just looked *so* good! Enter, finally, the dish towels—so instead of waiting for the shells to cool (so tedious), we could continue with our instant gratification, with well-swaddled hands.

Further on the subject of grill safety, there's a school of thought that the shellfish should be covered with wet burlap, to contain any sudden bursts of scalding oyster innards that, according to Cape Cod legend, could put your eye out. We suppose this might be possible, but we've never seen it (and in fact our oysters usually behave quite the opposite way, creaking open very slowly) and think it can be thwarted by good old-fashioned paying attention.

Study Says: No Shucking Way

We'd heard a rumor that shucking the oysters *before* grilling was the way to go, to get more smoky flavor in there. We were skeptical, so Tamara conducted an experiment (in Anchorage, Alaska, no less). Two dozen oysters had their top shells removed and were set on the grill in just their bottom shells, like an open-face sandwich, with a little mignonette on them—"to simmer in the flavor," as one dinner attendee suggested. And two dozen oysters were grilled closed, the way we've always done it. The open oysters were charred and dried out, while the closed ones were plump, tender and perfectly cooked, because they told us they were done by opening their shells! Less work, *and* better in the end.

When the hot oysters come off the grill, drop them directly onto the adjacent table. The person there can finish opening them with the oyster knife and dish towel (the shells will already be gaping a bit, and should pop open easily), and cut loose the little valve holding the flesh to the shell. Then drizzle the waiting oyster with mignonette, a squeeze of lemon or hot sauce. The chill of the topping will counteract the heat of the oyster, so people can slip them right into their little mouths, and drop the empty shells in the nearby trash can. The ballet of this constant motion—on the grill, off the grill, open, drizzle, slurp, drop—is beautiful in and of itself, and feeds people at whatever pace they want to be fed.

Note: To roast oysters in the oven, you'll need a large, deep tray (what's known as a hotel pan in restaurant lingo) or several baking dishes or roasting pans. Set a flat wire rack in each vessel, then fill with about an inch of water. Lay the oysters out on the racks, then set the trays in a 475°F oven for 7 or 8 minutes—the oysters should pop right open.

OYSTER TOPPINGS FOR EVERY GUEST

Good oysters and clams are delicious all by their naked selves, but to stimulate the appetite for more, you want to add a little variety with each bite. To this end, we usually make a classic mignonette—the very French standard oyster topping—and a more newfangled one, and put out Tabasco for people who want a bit of heat. Make the mignonettes at least an hour (and anywhere up to twenty-four hours) before you start grilling the oysters. This gives a little time for the shallots to mellow out. The prep for both is the same: Mix the ingredients together in a small bowl, taste for salt (remembering that good oysters will be briny on their own), *et voilà*.

FOR THE GUEST WHO IS . . .

...AN OLD WORLD TRADITIONALIST	...A NEW WORLD TRADITIONALIST	...A FUSION-HAPPY GOURMET
CLASSIC MIGNONETTE	**TABASCO SAUCE AND LEMONS**	**ASIAN MIGNONETTE**
Ingredients for 2¼ cups:	*Ingredients:*	*Ingredients for 2 cups:*
2 cups red wine vinegar	Tabasco sauce (or anything similar and vinegar-based—but nothing with habañero, as the oysters shouldn't have to suffer this way)	**1 cup rice wine vinegar**
1 teaspoon fresh lemon juice	Lemon wedges	**Juice from 2 limes (⅓ cup)**
4 or 5 small shallots, minced		**1 cucumber, peeled, seeded and coarsely grated**
Large pinch salt		**1 tablespoon granulated sugar**
Several grinds black pepper		**Large pinch salt**

WAX BEANS WITH ARUGULA

The play of the cold raw arugula and the warm cooked beans in this dish is a nice change of pace from standard salads, while still giving you all the green you need in your diet. The arugula and the herb dressing can be prepped a couple of hours ahead, but to keep the greens at their liveliest, wait to combine them and the warm beans until right before you serve. *Serves 8*

2 **big bunches fresh basil**

1 **big bunch fresh parsley**

3–5 **cloves garlic**

2 **lemons**

¼ **cup capers**

Salt and pepper

¾ **cup olive oil**

3½ **pounds green beans and/or yellow wax beans**

4 **bunches arugula**

Rinse the basil and parsley well and pick the leaves off their stems. Peel the garlic cloves and chop them into quarters. Squeeze the juice from 1 lemon. Add these to the bowl of a food processor or a blender along with the capers, a couple of large pinches of salt and a few grinds of pepper. Pulse a few times to chop the herbs, then, with the machine running, slowly drizzle in the olive oil. Check the resulting thin paste for balance—it should be very bright-tasting, with noticeable acid from the capers and lemon juice. (If you don't have a food processor, you can also chop everything up by hand—the rougher texture has its own merits. But take special care to mince the garlic very fine, or squeeze it through a garlic press, so it gets properly dispersed in the sauce.)

Set a large pot of salted water on to boil; add 1 tablespoon salt or so. While the water is heating, snap the stem ends off all of the beans, then wash and dry the arugula thoroughly. Arrange the arugula on a serving plate or in a large bowl. Squeeze half a lemon over the arugula and dust it with a pinch of salt (but go easy—the herb dressing has its own salt and lemon).

Boil the beans for just 2 minutes. They'll maintain a lot of their crunch, which is exactly what you want. After straining them, put them right back in the hot, empty pot, dump all of the herb mixture over and toss to coat well.

Scatter the hot green-bean business over the arugula. The heat of the beans will cause the arugula to wilt a little—just what you want to happen. Serve relatively promptly.

POTATO SALAD WITH BACON

Potato salad *kills*. We mean that in a good way, not in a mayonnaise-festering-on-a-buffet way. We mean that potato salad, especially this one (which is mayo-free, incidentally), is always a hit with the slavering crowds. You want nice creamy, dense potatoes: Yukon golds, Red Bliss or any of the fingerling varieties. *Serves 15–20*

8 pounds potatoes

2 pounds bacon

¾ cup olive oil

1½ cups red wine or cider vinegar

¼ cup whole-grain mustard

2 cloves garlic

Salt and pepper

6 scallions

2 bunches parsley

Set a large pot of heavily salted water on to boil. Scrub your potatoes well—no need to peel—and cut them into sixths or eighths, depending on the size—you want them in roughly ½-inch chunks. Set a cast-iron skillet or two over medium-low heat and lay out the bacon (or use the oven-baking method described on page 173). Let it cook, flipping occasionally, until it's nicely browned but not too crispy.

While the water is heating and the bacon is sizzling, combine the oil, vinegar and mustard in a jar with a tight-fitting lid. Squeeze the garlic cloves through a press or mash them to a pulp, and add them to the jar. Add a couple of large pinches of salt and a few generous grinds of pepper. Screw on the lid and shake vigorously to combine. (If you're thinking this is just a bigger, slightly skewed version of the dressing on page 65, you're right—see how versatile?)

Boil the potatoes for 12–15 minutes, until tender—poke a fork into one, and it should slide right off. If you're not sure, let them go a few more minutes—in this case, it's better to have them a bit soft and crumbly (and more amenable to soaking up the dressing) than too firm.

While the potatoes are boiling, chop up your scallions (white and green parts) into thin rings and roughly chop your parsley. Tear the bacon into bite-size bits.

Pour all the hot water off the potatoes, then put them back on the burner in the dry pan for about 10 seconds, shaking them a bit, just to dry them out a little more. Take the pan off the heat and dump the dressing over the hot potatoes, then add the scallions, parsley and bacon. Stir gently to combine, taking care not to mash up the potatoes too much. Transfer the salad to a serving bowl and, if you have room in your refrigerator, chill it for a bit. If not, it's fine to leave out (covered, to keep prying fingers off the bacon). Taste before serving—the flavors will change as the salad sits, and you may want to add more salt and vinegar.

Bacon, Big-Time

For prepping bacon on a grand scale, the best approach is to lay out all the slices on a couple of parchment- or wax paper–lined baking sheets (they must have rims!), stick them in the oven, then turn the oven to 400°F (don't preheat—the gradual temperature rise gives the fat a chance to render slowly). The bacon should be done to a good crispy-chewy texture in 25–30 minutes. If you have only one good baking sheet, place the slices in layers separated with additional sheets of parchment (you can prep this ahead of time and stow it in the fridge). When the top layer of bacon is done, scoop it off with tongs, peel off the parchment below and stick the pan back in the oven to brown up the next layer. Before you get to the bottom layer, you'll probably need to drain off the collected fat. Have an empty can handy, as well as some sturdy oven mitts; it's safest to place the can on the floor, then lower the tray, rather than hoist the sizzling fat up to counter height.

Veggie variation: Nothing really compares to bacon. But you can make an equally good, if different, meat-free potato salad by replacing the bacon with 4 or 5 celery stalks, chopped into little crunchy bits, to give a good contrasting texture with the soft potatoes. Then conjure the ghost of the absent bacon with smoked Spanish sweet paprika (not the hot stuff). Start with 1 heaping teaspoon mixed in with the dressing, then sprinkle on more at the end if you find you want a richer smoky taste.

GRILLED TOMATOES

Alongside the oysters, feel free to grill some tomatoes. The hot flames give a good char, which acts as a smoky foil to the tomatoes' sweetness in the height of summer. If you're doing the oysters in the oven rather than on the grill, lay the tomato slices out on a baking sheet and stick it under the broiler for 8–10 minutes. And if you're making this menu any other time than the summer tomato season, do the next recipe—Roasted Grape Tomatoes—instead. Cut ripe **tomatoes** (one per person, plus a few more) in half crosswise, set them in a bowl and drizzle with a generous amount of **olive oil.** Place the tomato halves on the grill and cook until the skins are blistered and charred, and the flesh is softened but not totally squishy, about 10 minutes—though it depends greatly on how hot your fire is. Set out on a large platter and sprinkle with **salt** and **pepper.**

ROASTED GRAPE TOMATOES

The no-grill, winter-chill way to get a little red in your diet. Tiny grape tomatoes are the only kind of fresh tomatoes we'll buy in the off-season, and roasting to caramelize them and concentrate their flavors makes them taste *almost* like summer. The herbs are nice—and a handy way to use up extras you may have lying around—but not vital. *Serves 15–20*

24 cloves garlic (or so)

12 pints grape tomatoes (see note)

A few sprigs fresh rosemary and/or thyme (optional)

Olive oil

Salt and pepper

Preheat the oven to 375°F. Peel and lightly crush the garlic. Toss it in a large bowl with the tomatoes and herbs, plus just enough oil to coat the tomatoes—a large glug is ample. Spread the tomatoes and herbs out evenly—ideally in a single layer—in several baking pans or rimmed cookie sheets and set them in a 375°F oven for 30–40 minutes, checking them from time to time and shaking them around in the pans a little to keep them from sticking. Pull them out when they're soft and the skins are a bit shriveled.

Notes:
- When buying grape tomatoes, get the ripest you can find, but check the bottom of each pint box to make sure there are no moldy ones.
- You can roast the tomatoes hours ahead and serve them at room temperature, or stick them in the oven as you're preheating it for the oysters. Leftovers also taste great in an omelet or scrambled eggs the next morning, especially if you're a little hung over.
- For a more substantial side dish, toss in about ½ pound good firm goat cheese, cut into large cubes. Don't stir the tomatoes while they're baking, then slide everything gently onto a plate to serve, keeping the cheese relatively intact.

PEACH COBBLER

This is a favorite dessert of ours—straightforward, rustic-looking and versatile. We most often use peaches (as here), but you could use plums, nectarines, berries, or, later in the year, apples or pears. Whatever you choose, get fruit that's as ripe as possible. For peaches, that means they should be fragrant and soft. Firm peaches are all too common—but you can pick up promising ones several days before you plan to use them and let them ripen in a paper bag on a sunny windowsill.

For the topping, we owe Millicent Souris, the most accomplished pastry chef we know. She has the fabled Magic Hands that turn out perfect pie crusts and other baked goodies every time. So, even though we wrote down her biscuit recipe word for word, it just never turns out quite as splendidly as when she does it. But maybe you'll discover you have the golden touch? Even if not, though, the results will be delicious. Try to stash at least one serving away for later—it's particularly excellent with your first cup of coffee in the morning. *Serves 15–20*

For Millicent's biscuit topping:

1¼ cups (2½ sticks) unsalted butter, chilled, plus more for greasing the pan

4 cups all-purpose flour, plus more for dusting the pan

3 teaspoons salt

5 teaspoons baking powder

1 cup plus 1–2 tablespoons buttermilk

3–4 tablespoons granulated sugar

For the filling:

24 medium peaches

1 cup granulated or light brown sugar

1 teaspoon salt

1 heaping teaspoon ground cinnamon

½ teaspoon ground nutmeg

¼ teaspoon ground allspice

¼ teaspoon ground ginger

5 tablespoons butter, chilled and cut into 16 pieces

¼ cup dark rum

1 lemon

Preheat the oven to 450°F and butter a 12-by-16-inch baking pan (or two or three equivalent smaller ones). In a large bowl, sift together the flour, salt and baking powder.

Cut the butter into small cubes. Using a pastry blender, two knives or your fingers (but only if you have very cold hands), work the butter into the flour until the mix is the texture of clumpy sand. (If using a food processor, pulse four or five times.) Slowly add 1 cup buttermilk, stirring with a wooden spoon to form a wet dough. (With a fo-pro, just pulse briefly to combine.) You may need to add more buttermilk—up to another 2 tablespoons—to make the dough hold together and be just a bit sticky. Stash the dough, still in its bowl, in the refrigerator while you prepare the fruit.

Wash and slice the fruit and toss it into a large mixing bowl—big enough to get your hands in and mix all the fruit with the sugar, salt, cinnamon, nutmeg, allspice, ginger, butter and rum. Squeeze the lemon over and toss thoroughly. Pour the fruit into the baking pan(s) and let the whole mess rest for about 15 minutes.

On a lightly floured board or countertop, roll out your biscuit dough lightly or pat it out with your cold hands (dust a little flour on the rolling pin or your hands as well, as the dough will still be sticky). Don't work too hard—just roll it out enough to combine the fat a little more, until the dough is about 1 inch thick. Then pull off chunks of dough with your hands—misshapen, various sizes, whatever—and drop them on top of the fruit to cover it evenly. Sprinkle a little sugar over the top, then slide the pan into the oven. Check after 20 minutes; the biscuits should have risen, and the tops should be browning a bit. As soon as they've browned a little, pull the heat back to 350°F, cover the pan with foil and bake for another 10 minutes or so. Before pulling the cobbler out, check that the undersides of the biscuits are cooked: Lift up the edge of one—it should be soft and flaky inside, and not at all doughy. If necessary, give it more time in 4-minute increments or so.

Notes:

- The cobbler can be made hours or even a day ahead. If you go the latter route, cover it with foil and stash it somewhere cool—but do not refrigerate unless it's August and you don't have air conditioning. Reheat for about 5 minutes in a 400°F oven before serving, to revive the biscuits.
- Tamara takes another shortcut by replacing the spices with 1 tablespoon premixed pumpkin pie spice plus another ½ teaspoon cinnamon.

THE AMAZING CASSOULET

Cassoulet may just be French for "pork and beans," but it is still an extraordinary concoction. A slow-cooked pot full of melting-soft white beans and assorted mystery meats, cassoulet is way up there in the culinary firmament, one of those elaborate dishes that is so swaddled in lore, regional rivalry and animal fat that it's like the Everest of cooking: intimidating—and tantalizing—for anyone up to a challenge.

So of course Tamara wanted to make it. Never mind that neither of us had tasted "real" cassoulet, in its natural habitat in the Languedoc region in southwestern France. At that point, Tamara had never even been to France, and had sampled cassoulet only once, twenty-five years before, when her master-chef grandfather had made it as a dinner special at the Sun City Country Club in Phoenix, Arizona. And Zora had a distinct disdain for the fetishization of French food, partly because the cassoulets she'd eaten in restaurants didn't seem much more than, well, pork and beans. But we figured, in a spiteful riposte to the previous year's "freedom fries" bullshit, a French bean monstrosity would be the *perfect* thing to serve to our guests at Election Day Café 2004.

Unlike our regular Sunday Night Dinners, Election Day Café, which we run whenever there's a big race going, is an open, no-set-numbers, just-show-up event. In 2004, we basically poured all our political frustrations into one long day of cooking our asses off for active members of our great democracy, as more than sixty friends dropped by after visiting their polling stations. We started early in the morning for the before-work voters, with crispy yeasted waffles and chicken-fried steak with country gravy. We took a little nap, and then made an all-American diner lunch of tomato soup and grilled cheese sandwiches.

And for dinner, we rolled out the cassoulet. Good thing, too, as poll returns dragged on till the wee hours; the rich, hearty beans kept our blood sugar stable and our political arguments relatively rational. The cassoulet was proof that excellent food can turn even a grim day into a memorably good one—and that if we really want to get out the vote, maybe we should reward people with duck fat. (Despite the cassoulet's success in 2004, we didn't serve it again for Election Day Café 2008—we just didn't want to jinx ourselves. We guess it worked.)

So if you want to reward your own friends and neighbors for anything, cassoulet is just the thing. And if you want to conquer your fear of getting your kitchen greasy, this is also just the thing. Like so many one-pot meals, the actual cooking doesn't take a lot of skill or attention. But the process takes time, and serious organization. This is no three-hour tour.

In fact, cassoulet is more like a three-*day* project—ideally spread out over the course of a week or so (for reasons we'll get to). It involves many kinds of fat and meat, and just looking at the list can be frightening if you haven't yet mentally prepared yourself. The best preparation, actually, is to imagine yourself as a cranky, thrifty French farm wife who really wants to guard against the winter cold seeping through the walls of her centuries-old stone house. This will give you a better grip on why there are so many odd pieces of meat. Cassoulet is a way of infusing boring old beans with real meaty substance, by using all the bits of the animals that farm-wife-you preserved in your pantry a couple of months back: sausages, salt pork and duck confit may not be prime cuts, but they are all uncommonly tasty.

You may be tempted to save some time by buying confit duck legs—but your inner cranky French lady would consider that a waste of money. And she'd also think it's a little like sex without the foreplay (and she would know—there's a direct correlation between using duck fat and getting laid). The modern-day, not-French part of you will of course appreciate the meat-drunk praise you'll receive and the deep and lasting sense of personal accomplishment you'll feel.

We Frenchified our brains by reading Julia Child (helpful, exact instructions) and *Larousse Gastronomique* (no measurements, loads of random lore and village-against-village arguments). What we took away from this was a feeling of great relief that there was no one "right" way to make cassoulet—to the point where even we can't agree on a single recipe. Just as Castelnaudary, Carcassonne and Toulouse bicker over goose fat and partridges, Tamara and Zora have their separate visions of what makes a really tasty cassoulet, so we've laid out our preferences alongside the ingredients. You should pick and choose what sounds good to you—and that should be your ultimate guiding light when you're feeling a little unsteady on Day Three of the Great Cassoulet Expedition.

Alongside, you should definitely avail yourself of something cranky old French ladies snowbound in the Pyrenees probably do not have: a green salad. As we've lectured plenty of times earlier in this book, a good fresh salad is the best antidote to fat—and cassoulet represents perhaps the most animal fat you can consume in a single meal. If you're up to it, you can also serve some braised celery hearts and radishes on the side—their soft flavor is refreshingly clean. For dessert, if anyone can muster it (we served a killer three-layer cake at Election Day Café—but we can't recommend it, because then we'd feel responsible for your death), you can make a quickie little *pain d'épices*—which is just French for "gingerbread."

A note on quantities: The cassoulet recipe we give here—and all the side dishes—will serve eight with some leftovers, or even ten, so long as your guests are not gripped with winter cold or political anxiety. Certainly don't waste the cassoulet on fewer people than eight—you'll want to share the love, and get the praise for your days of labor. And if you want to serve more, by all means, double or triple the recipe—but you'll get better results if you then get two or three separate pots going, rather than lumping everything into a giant tub. (We find the basic recipe fits snugly in a 5-quart enameled cast-iron pot.)

THE AMAZING CASSOULET

- Choose-Your-Own-Adventure Cassoulet
- Escarole with Roasted Pears and Pomegranate Seeds
- Braised Celery and Radishes
- Orange Gingerbread

Plan of Attack:

1 week out:

1. Shop for everything.

2. Salt duck.

6 days out:

Confit duck.

2 days out:

Soak beans.

1 day out:

1. Cook beans.

2. Prepare additional meats.

3. Assemble cassoulet and bake for 2–3 hours; chill overnight.

Show day:

1. Bake cassoulet another 2 hours.

2. Braise celery and radishes.

3. Measure out gingerbread ingredients.

4. Assemble green salad.

5. Take cassoulet out of oven; put gingerbread in.

6. Serve dinner to thunderous applause.

7. Offer around wafer-thin slices of gingerbread.

Drink Up!

Cassoulet is so very French that we first want to send you toward the wonderful wines of southwest France, the area where the dish was born. Madiran, Cahors, Corbières, Saint Chinian, even a cheaper Bordeaux if you want to be fancy—these are all work-horse country wines with a tannic edge that will cut through all that duck fat, not unlike the way an opera singer's stridency cuts through the orchestra. Other country wines like malbec, syrah and cabernet sauvignon will do as well, but for a dish so steeped in regional history, it is nice to taste the marriage that was meant to be.

LEARN FROM OUR MISTAKES!

Close Up the Duck Chop Shop

When she was in her most nose-to-tail phase, Zora spent a day butchering several whole duck carcasses (nabbed from the live-poultry operation at the end of her block), freezing the breasts, making stock and pâté and rendering the fat, which she used to confit all the legs. She felt proud and stocked for the winter—but her kitchen floor was shiny and slippery for weeks. And worse, the smell of duck, initially delicious, had permeated the entire apartment. She woke in the night, queasy and surrounded by duck aroma, and feeling like she never wanted to eat again. Now she limits her duck prep to one activity a day—one day for confit, another for stock—with plenty of ventilation in the kitchen during and after. She even, when necessary, buys duck fat from the butcher, to spare herself the overly ducky smells from rendering it.

Unfortunately, the duck fat will likely be one of the more expensive components of your cassoulet investment, but you may be able to cut a deal like Tamara did: She bought 10 pounds from the butcher and kept it in their freezer, as her private stash. In any case, it's worth the money—it's a small price to pay for keeping your appetite primed for tasty, tasty duck.

CHOOSE-YOUR-OWN-ADVENTURE CASSOULET

The essentials of a cassoulet are simply white beans, odd bits of meat and time. Oh, and garlic. OK, and we really think you have to have duck confit—it's the decadent element that makes this worth inviting people over for. But what kind of beans, which meats and how you answer the great bread-crumb dilemma are all entirely up to you. Tailor your cassoulet to your tastes and what ingredients you can easily come by—sure, put in some legwork in the shopping, but save your energy for the kitchen. As we also mentioned earlier, the ideal timeline for cassoulet cooking is at least a week. Partly this is for the sake of the duck confit—letting it age a bit in the fridge improves its flavor significantly. Even more important, though, it's for your mental health: Spreading the work out over a week gives you a chance to clean up your kitchen, get a grip on the next task and clear the air (see page 182).

Confit has its own mystique, but it's really just a process of cooking duck legs (or anything, really) submerged entirely in fat, for a long time in a slow oven. And that "for a long time in a slow oven" part means you barely have to lift a finger. Duck legs are traditionally used for confit, but we use a whole duck, as that's usually easier to come by (and a bit cheaper) than legs alone.

As for the beans, the French could fill a book on the prickly subject. (You don't hear them singing, "Beans, beans, the musical fruit"—beans are *serious* business!) But that certainly doesn't mean you have to use French beans; we suggest a few other varieties. Feel free to get creative, but stick with white beans. Finally: the meats. There are some strange scraps in here, but each piece serves a function. We outline the key elements in the ingredients list, along with suggestions for substitutions. Again, think creatively—one of our cassoulet informants even swears by rabbit, as it adds a crucial lightness to what can be a gut-buster of a dish. The critical element, though, is variety, both in texture and flavor—you want each bite of the cassoulet to be a little different. Top-quality sausage really makes a difference, but go for the cheapest cuts in everything else. *Serves 8–10*

THE AMAZING CASSOULET

FOR THE CONFIT	COMMENTS
Legs, thighs and breasts from 1 whole duck (about 4½ pounds), or 4 duck legs, thighs attached	Moulard duck is preferable, as it's the fattiest and cooks fastest, but Pekin is also good. Avoid Muscovy ducks if you can, as they're much leaner; if it's all you can get, plan for a couple hours' more cooking time.
¼ cup salt, or thereabouts	You want about 1 tablespoon, or a bit more, per piece of meat
Pepper **5 or 6 cloves garlic, smashed** **Small handful fresh thyme sprigs**	
1–1½ cups duck fat	In a pinch, you can use olive oil or very good-quality lard, but then you won't have a trove of pure—and reusable—duck fat at the end of the process.

FOR THE BEANS	COMMENTS
4 cups (1½ pounds) dried white beans	Flageolet and tarbais are the French standards, but great northern or navy beans are just fine. Tamara votes for cannellini beans; Zora's favorite are gigantes, the Greek-style giant lima beans. Regardless, get the freshest—compare sell-by dates on the bags.
1 pound fresh pork skin	Also called fresh pork rind, this adds a lovely silkiness to the bean broth—and it's dirt cheap. Ask your butcher, or look for it on the fringes of the pork section of your supermarket.
1 fresh ham hock	Another flavor enhancer; a trotter (foot) will work as well. Try to avoid smoked or otherwise heavily cured hocks, as the flavor is too strong. And barring all that, any big pork bone with a little meat attached is better than nothing.
2 medium yellow onions	
10 whole cloves	It's hard to discern their flavor in the final product, but it's a great way to use up these malingerers of the spice rack if you have them. If you don't, skip 'em.
6 cloves garlic	Oh, don't worry—there will be even more later. . . .
Small bunch fresh thyme **3 or 4 bay leaves** **Salt**	

FOR THE MEATS	COMMENTS
Duck fat	You'll certainly have some left from your confit project—no need to buy extra.
1 pound pork sausages	Garlicky fresh sausages are key. Good ideas: Polish kielbasa; an Italian job without fennel; not-too-smoky andouille. Bad idea: maple-cured anything. Best idea: homemade—see note on page 191.
1 pound meat	Whatever you like, and make it the cheap cuts. Lamb lends earthiness; Tamara prefers more pork. Beef is unremarkable. Venison would probably kick ass. You could even just get another variety of sausage.
⅓ pound pancetta	Pancetta is cured pork belly—like bacon, but not smoked. If you can't get it, look for fatback, but, even though it hurts to type this, don't substitute bacon, as the smoky flavor can take over the dish.
2 yellow onions	
15 cloves garlic	Yes, that much. In fact, what the heck, why not throw in those last few cloves and make it an even head?
2 or 3 carrots—or none	Tamara: [*shudder*] "I hate carrots." Zora: "Thank the fucking Lord! A vegetable! More, please!"
3–6 whole peeled tomatoes (fresh or canned)	Some purists don't use them. We think they add a bit of acid and sweetness that's helpful—and Zora leans toward the generous end.
3 tablespoons tomato paste	Only if you're already pro-tomato.
1 cup white wine or dry vermouth	Don't think we'd get into a one-week project without some booze.
1 cup duck stock	Make this with the leftover bits from your confit carcass. Or use ½ cup of the "duck jelly" left over from the confit (see page 188), plus some water.
Salt and pepper	

THE AMAZING CASSOULET

FOR THE ASSEMBLY	COMMENTS
5 or 6 bacon slices	Tamara can't help working in a dab of bacon—she just uses it to line the pot. If you've used pork skin in the beans, you can use it instead—though we like it more for what it adds to the dish than as an ingredient itself.
Whole fresh nutmeg	A small detail that makes a big difference—freshly grated nutmeg is a world away from the preground stuff, so don't cut corners here.
Fresh thyme	If you used it all up in the beans, that's OK. But if you do have some left, why not add it?
1 cup fresh bread crumbs, from 5 or 6 slices good white bread	Tamara: "Heresy!" Zora: "Essential textural contrast!"
Big handful fresh parsley	Only if you choose the bread-crumb path.

Prepare the duck confit: If you don't have a nice butcher to chop your duck up for you, do it yourself: You want the breasts, legs and thighs off the carcass, ideally with the bones. Remember that it will all be somewhat shredded at the end, so you don't have to be too tidy—get in there with the poultry shears and your sharpest knife (a boner, if you've got one—heh). Set aside the wings and the back for making duck stock, per the directions on page 63. (Do it today, or stash the pieces in the freezer for later; either way, don't waste this stuff—duck stock is culinary gold, and you can even use some later in the recipe.) Generously salt and pepper your duck pieces all over and set them in the heaviest pot you have with a tight-fitting lid. Narrow and deep is preferable to wide and shallow, as snugger-fitting meat requires less duck fat to cover—a cast-iron Dutch oven is good. Scatter the garlic and thyme in between and on top. Put the lid on and refrigerate the thing for at least 12 hours and up to 24.

The next day, preheat the oven to 225°F and pull out your duck fat to let it get to a runny state (you can warm it on low heat if you like). Pull out the duck pieces and brush off the salt, discard the garlic and thyme and pour off any liquid in the pot. Nestle the duck back in the heavy pot, layering the pieces to create as even a surface as possible. Pour the fat over the pieces to completely cover them—or at least up to the very edge of the skin and any exposed bones. The fat on the duck will render as it cooks, which will give you a little extra coverage. Stick the lid on the pot and place it in the oven. Go about your business for 3 hours or so. By then, the meat should be falling off the bone and easily pierced with a toothpick—or the legs should, at least; the breasts will never quite reach the same tenderness. (Note, though, that Pekin ducks typically take an hour longer than Moulards.) When the duck is done, pull it out and let it cool.

Stash the whole thing in the fridge, covered, until next week. The fat will congeal into a solid, which you can then scrape off and save to use later in the recipe. (Freeze the rest for other projects, such as the most delicious roasted potatoes you'll ever eat, or the Grilled Peaches with Duck Fat on page 108.) At the bottom of the pot will be super-savory "duck jelly," congealed, concentrated stock that you can use later in the recipe.

Make the beans: Two nights before your meal, pick through the beans and toss any shriveled or broken ones, and set the rest to soak in plenty of water. The next day, drain the beans and set them in a large, heavy stockpot. In a separate small saucepan, put the pork skin in water to cover and boil for 15 minutes or so, until it's soft and flexible. While that's going, toss your ham hock in with the beans. Peel your onions, then stick the whole cloves into the outside; place these in the pot along with the garlic cloves (unpeeled is fine), thyme

Duck parts, salted and waiting for the confit treatment

THE AMAZING CASSOULET

sprigs and bay leaves. (If you're feeling tidy, you can tie the sprigs in a bundle.) Add enough water to cover everything by about 1 inch (past the first knuckle on your finger). Bring to a boil and skim off any scum that rises to the top, then turn the heat way down and let the beans simmer very gently for about 40 minutes, until they're tender but not falling apart (the total cooking time will depend greatly on how old your beans are). When they're done, add salt to taste, then drain the beans, saving the liquid. Discard the onion, set aside the ham hocks and pull out the garlic cloves—squeeze the garlic out of its skin, and mix it in with the beans. If you have an inborn taste for gummy, chewy things, set aside the pork skin—we have a treat for you in a bit. When the ham hocks are cool, pick off whatever meat you can and add it to the beans.

Prepare the meats: While the beans are simmering away, take out the duck confit to come to room temperature. Cut up your assorted meats into 1-inch or so chunks, and chop the pancetta into small cubes. Scrape a big spoonful of duck fat off the top of the confit and put it in a heavy pot on medium-high heat. Fry up the sausages and whatever meat you're using—work in batches, and give them plenty of time so all sides are nice and brown. While they're browning, chop the onions roughly and peel all the garlic, crushing it as you go. (Tamara likes to whiz these up in the food processor with a smidge of water to make a thick paste.) Peel your carrots, if using, and cut them into ½-inch chunks—not too small, or they'll get totally lost in the stew. When the meat is browned, take it out of the pot and set it aside; slice up the sausage into bite-size pieces and keep it separate from the other meats. Put the pancetta in the pot and stir as it browns.

When it's done, leave it in the pot, but add a dab more duck fat and toss in the onions and the carrots, if using; stir and fry on medium heat until the onions just start to soften, about 3 minutes. Then add the garlic and fry for another minute or so. (If you're starting with an onion-garlic paste but want carrots too, fry the paste down first, till the liquid cooks away, then add the carrots.) Add the tomatoes, if your heart desires, crushing them roughly with your hand; add the tomato paste too, if using. Pour in the wine and quickly scrape up the browned bits from the bottom of the pot; add the duck stock, or scrape out some of the duck jelly from the confit pot. Return all of the meat—but not the sausage—and give everything a good stir. Add salt to taste (go easy if you've used the duck jelly), along with a bit of black pepper. Put the lid on the pot, turn the heat to low and let it simmer for

Assembling the cassoulet Tamara's way, with bacon lining the pot

1 hour or so, stirring a few times just to make sure nothing's sticking.

Your beans will probably be done before the meat stew is. Perfect—this gives you a little time to sort your confit: Pull each piece out of the pot, scraping as much fat off as possible. Pull off the skin and discard it, along with the bones. Break all the duck meat into 1-inch or so chunks. At this point, you'll probably want to repackage the remaining duck fat in something you can stash in the freezer; same goes for any remaining duck jelly.

Once that's all done and the sauce in the meat has thickened up nicely, turn off the heat, tidy up, wipe the grease off your stove and have a drink. The hard work is behind you.

Assemble the cassoulet: Preheat the oven to 350°F. Get out your chosen heavy-bottomed pot. At this point, the purest French cut the pork skin from the beans up in little pieces, and place the bits all over the bottom of the pot. They like the squidgy, fatty texture—to each his own comfort food, we suppose. It's not ours, though. Zora hates to see things go to waste, so she keeps the hunks of skin large and lays them on the bottom of the pot, to give the beans something to rest on (and tries to avoid scooping out the hunks when serving). Tamara prefers to line the bottom of the pot with bacon slices (uncooked) and scatter a few pinches of pepper over them. But you could also go without any pot liner at all.

From there, gently spoon a third of the cooked, drained beans into the pot. Layer on half of your assorted meats—duck confit, sausage pieces and the stew with all its sauce. Grate a light dusting of nutmeg over the meat and strip the leaves off a couple of thyme sprigs if you still have them and toss them in. Repeat with another third of the beans and the remaining meat—though you may wind up not using all of the duck, no matter how hard you try. Top with the last of the beans and grate over a little more nutmeg. Finally, pour the reserved bean liquid in, until the beans are just covered. (Save any extra liquid for adding later.)

Place the pot in the oven, uncovered, and bake for about 1 hour, until the liquid begins to simmer and a little crust forms on the top of the beans. Gently press the crust under the liquid with the back of a spoon and reduce the heat to 275°F. Check it in another 45 minutes or so, breaking the crust and stirring it back in. If the whole mess starts to look dry below the surface, add more bean liquid. After a little more than 2 hours, pull the pot out and let it cool; cover and refrigerate overnight. Save any remaining bean liquid too. (If you don't have the luxury of the overnight rest, then just carry on with the crust-cracking and liquid-checking for another 2–3 hours. Drinks, and a good book, are in order.)

The next day, about 3 hours before you plan to eat, preheat the oven to 350°F and take the cassoulet out of the refrigerator. Uncover the pot and pour in enough reserved bean stock (or warm water) to just cover the beans—about 1 cup. After about 30 minutes, turn the heat down to 300°F and break the crust again. While you're here, check the liquid—it should be runny enough to serve in a bowl, but not as thin as a brothy soup. If you're heading toward thick, don't be afraid to add a little more liquid. Total cooking time will be 2 hours or so, or until you've got the rest of the dinner done.

At this point, reader, you must make one final choice. . . .

If you choose to follow in the footsteps of Tamara, leave the last gorgeously golden crust that forms intact. Pull the pot from the oven and let it rest for 15 minutes while you pull the rest of the dinner together and get people seated. Break the crust at the table, inducing oohs and aahs.

THE END

If you choose to follow in the footsteps of Zora, rinse your parsley and chop it up fine, then toss it with the bread crumbs, which you've whizzed up in the blender. Sprinkle the mix on top of the cassoulet, dipping your spoon into the fat on top of the beans and drizzling this over. Crank the oven to 500°F for 5 minutes, then pull the toasted beauty out. Let it sit for a few minutes, and serve to acclaim.

THE END

Notes:

- For the overachievers in the house, may we suggest making your own sausage? This book would collapse under the weight of the cassoulet if we included instructions here; instead, we direct you to Julia Child's *Mastering the Art of French Cooking,* which has an easy recipe for Toulouse-style sausage in patties (no casings required), though we suggest a bit more garlic, and pancetta instead of straight fat. You can pull this off even if you don't have a meat grinder—describe your project to your butcher, and they'll be happy to grind the meat for you. You can also chop the meat fine, then whiz it briefly in your food processor— even though Julia would probably not approve.

- If you make the confit more than a week ahead, for safety's sake take it out of its original pot and repack it. This is easiest if you chill it, then scrape off the fat and the duck jelly, keeping them separate. Shred the meat and repack it in a clean container where it all fits snugly; press down to get out the air bubbles, then pour the duck fat over. This will keep in the fridge for a good month.

Yes, Chef!

If you have the good fortune of knowing a professional cook—whether a line cook or someone who goes by Chef at work—*do not hesitate* to invite him or her for a home-cooked meal. Don't let yourself be intimidated. Because no one ever cooks for these people, they are quite often thrilled to be served in the same way they serve others. Resist the urge to ask for their help, however. It's the same as asking advice from a doctor at a cocktail party.

ESCAROLE WITH ROASTED PEARS AND POMEGRANATE SEEDS

When Sunday Night Dinner guests ask very, very nicely, we serve a version of this salad with candied bacon (as on page 134). We *do not* recommend you do the same when serving it with cassoulet, even if your friends beg. The double-pork whammy could really do them in. What you really need here are the greens—and you could use watercress, arugula, whatever in lieu of the escarole. We just think escarole doesn't get enough play. For eight people, slice 3 **pears** in small wedges, drizzle with a tiny bit of olive oil and place on a cookie sheet; roast at 400°F until browned, 25–30 minutes, then set aside to cool. Wash 1 large head **escarole,** dry it well and tear the leaves into a large salad bowl. Toss in the seeds from half a **pomegranate.** Make a dressing of ¼ cup **olive oil,** 2 tablespoons **sherry vinegar,** a large handful of crushed **pomegranate seeds** and just a pinch of **salt** and **pepper;** shake vigorously in a jar. Add the cooled pears to the escarole, pour the dressing over and toss.

Feed the Masses—but Check Your Watch

Doubling, tripling or even sextupling a recipe for a crowd can require a little more than straight-up times tables. Zora once decided to make fresh pasta for a crowd of twenty-five. She dutifully multiplied the flour and eggs—but totally failed to multiply the time required to process six times the usual amount of pasta. Fortunately, she'd gotten an early start—because she spent three hours cranking the pasta through her machine. (Her abs were sore for days afterward.) So always take time into account—even if it's just a question of washing double the amount of salad greens.

BRAISED CELERY AND RADISHES

Because cassoulet is so old-school, it seems only fitting to dust off some less-than-trendy vegetables to go alongside. You may not think of celery and radishes as anything more than vehicles for packaged onion-soup dip, but when you simmer them with a little bit of stock and wine, they're positively refreshing. The radishes turn a twee shade of pink, but they stay a tiny bit spicy. This is probably the most delicate and subtle dish in this whole book—enjoy it while you can! *Serves 8–10*

2 bunches celery

2 bunches radishes

4 tablespoons (½ stick) butter

½ cup chicken stock or water

Dry vermouth or very dry white wine

Small handful fresh thyme sprigs

Salt and pepper

Trim off the root end of the celery and the top leaves, and rinse the stalks well—no need to dry. Cut the stalks crosswise, so you have 2- or 3-inch pieces. Scrub the radishes well, trim off the straggly roots and green tops and slice each one in half lengthwise.

Set a large, wide pot with a lid on medium-high heat and add the butter. When it has melted and foamed, add the celery and radishes and stir to coat all in butter. Then add the stock and the vermouth, plus the thyme sprigs and a pinch of salt and pepper. Put on the lid and turn the heat down to medium-low. Let simmer for 15–20 minutes, until the celery is soft but not mushy.

Remove the celery and radishes from the broth with tongs and set them on a serving platter. Turn the heat back up to high and let the remaining liquid boil down until slightly thickened. Pick out the thyme sprigs and pour the sauce over the plated vegetables. Serve hot.

> *Note:* If you have room in the oven, you can simply toss all the ingredients in a baking pan (cut the butter into small pieces), cover with foil and bake in a 350°F oven for 30 minutes. You can serve the vegetables dry or in the broth—or pour off the broth and boil it down on the stove top.

ORANGE GINGERBREAD

Wintry desserts are a challenge for us—it's slim pickings for fruit, and our other go-to, ice cream, isn't very appealing. Each year, we fail to remember gingerbread until just before the spring thaw—and then wish we'd been eating it the whole damn frozen-in time. This can be mixed together quickly, then baked during dinner. Unsweetened whipped cream will dress it up nicely, but that may be overkill following the cassoulet. It's also great served plain, right out of the oven. *Serves 8–10*

For the cake:

½ cup (1 stick) butter, plus more for greasing the pan

2½ cups all-purpose flour, plus more for dusting the pan

½ cup dark brown sugar

Zest from 2 oranges

1 teaspoon baking soda

½ teaspoon salt

1 tablespoon ground ginger

1½ teaspoons ground nutmeg (about half a whole nutmeg)

2 tablespoons candied ginger (optional)

½ cup molasses

1 cup milk

2 large eggs

For the glaze:

2 oranges

Granulated sugar

Preheat the oven to 350°F. Butter and flour a 5-by-9-inch loaf pan or a 9-by-9-inch baking pan. In a small saucepan, melt ½ cup butter over medium heat; remove from the heat and stir in the brown sugar and orange zest. In a medium bowl, combine the flour, baking soda, salt, ginger and nutmeg; stir with a fork or whisk to distribute the spices and baking soda. Chop up your candied ginger, if using, into small nuggets and toss them into the flour. In a large measuring cup, mix the molasses and milk.

By this time, your butter-sugar mixture should be a little cooler, and you can stir the eggs into that, whisking until the mixture is glossy. Pour this into the flour and stir briefly, then pour in the molasses and milk. Stir only just enough to combine—lumps are fine. Pour the batter into the pan and bake for 35–40 minutes, until a toothpick stuck in the center comes out with a few crumbs.

While the gingerbread is cooling on a rack, make the glaze: Squeeze the orange juice and measure—it should be about ½ cup. Add half as much granulated sugar and pour into a heavy nonreactive saucepan and heat to a boil. Let it simmer until just thickened, about 3 minutes. Poke the top of the cooled cake all over with a toothpick, then pour on the glaze.

OVER-THE-TOP MENU #4

THE MAGNIFICENT LAMB ROAST

A whole lamb, roasted on a spit, was something of a signature dish around the original Reynolds Ranch, as Tamara's first Queens apartment/community center/ recreational facility was known. The tradition started on New Year's Eve 2004, when Tamara's vision of a Hawaiian-theme pig roast soon doubled in scope. She'd drafted Peter to do the heavy porcine lifting, and, as a Greek American, he had his own way of ringing in the new year. He agreed to help with the pig, so long as he got to add a whole lamb on a spit to the menu.

When the main courses went mano a mano (hoof to hoof?), the lamb beat the socks off the pig (which, to be fair, was also quite succulent). Guests were thrilled, Peter was vindicated, and soon we were roasting lambs on spits at the drop of a hat. We did three more over the next year or so. Which isn't to say the initial process was a breeze.

In fact, the whole first lamb roast counts as one big LEARN FROM OUR MISTAKES. We'd invited more than thirty guests and had ordered a 30-pound pig and a 50-pound lamb (live weight). But the day before the party, after a week of poring over roasting schematics found on the Internet, Peter and Zora hadn't even managed to rig up a barbecue. Despite Tamara's assurances that we'd have plenty of side dishes ("and there's always booze!"), everyone was pretty tense. Finally, Peter tracked down a clean 50-gallon drum and got our sculptor friends Joel and Deb to slice it in half in their metal shop.

The day of the party, we were all set up—with *two* roasting animals on spits—on Tamara's front porch, which measured just 8 feet by 15 feet. According to city regulations, we should've been at least another 2 feet away from the building, but Tamara had set up big buckets of water and, as an extra precaution, baked cookies to placate the fire brigade, should it arrive to investigate. And we're surprised it didn't, considering our blunder with the flame itself. After looking in vain for proper charcoal in the dead of winter, we bought what we could find: a few neglected bags of mesquite in a corner of The Home Depot. We shouldn't have been surprised at how the chunks of wood (made for, duh, *smoking* meat) yielded a thick cloud of acrid, eye-searing smoke. We wept for the full five hours of roasting, and our clothes smelled like a campfire for weeks afterward.

Then the pig spit (supplied by the butcher) turned out to be too short to set in the rests on either side of the fire; this called for an emergency swap out to a longer broomstick, a messy business that required three people and prompted Deb to say, "This is kind of sexy, actually." To add to the panic, just hours before the thirty-odd guests were due to arrive, the pesky lamb began to slip on the spit. The imagery was a little ghastly, particularly this early in the roasting process, before the carcass was good and edible-looking. But with another 50 yards of twine wadded up in desperate knots, the thing finally stayed put firmly enough to toast each side evenly as we cranked. And so what if the guests arrived and the meat still had another few hours to cook? We had the rest of the year—which at this point, was roughly six hours—to serve the meal; a champagne-and-lamb toast could be festive, after all.

Despite the incorrect use of mesquite charcoal, the tiny cooking area, the broomstick as a spit, slipping meat problems, and an oil drum as a cooker, the meat was stupendously delicious—a little smoky, a little tangy, very moist. The strongest endorsement came from a surprise guest who really got into the primal fun of breaking down the meat. With the carcass splayed out on a bench behind her, Barbara happily gnawed on a greasy rib bone and rolled her eyes: "I can't believe I was a vegetarian for eight years!"

Fortunately, since our first foray into spit roasting, we've managed to streamline

THE MAGNIFICENT LAMB ROAST

the process (a little). We've gotten less insanely ambitious about the side dishes and desserts—no croquembouche (see page 215), that's for damn sure. Now we do bite-size dessert morsels of a far simpler kind (dates stuffed with almond paste is the option we offer here), and to go along with the meat, we throw out a few tasty salads and call it good. (All of the side-dish recipes in this menu are written to serve eight people—multiply as necessary.)

We're not going to lie to you: This is a *massive* undertaking. But it is also road-tested as something that totally unprepared people like ourselves can pull off. You can piggyback on our numerous mistakes, and avoid them. And consider this: Once you've gone through this trial by fire, every other outdoor-cooking project will be like sleepwalking.

Drink Up!

When you hear *lamb,* think *Lambrusco.* Not only is it a handy mnemonic, but Lambrusco has a certain retro charm that only sparkling wines can conjure. But this is no Riunite on ice—Lambrusco is at heart a dry red, with just a bit of sweet fruit straight out of the gate. And it's served chilled. And $15 will buy you an excellent bottle. And did we mention the bubbles? Talk about a festive end to a four-hour man-versus-beast competition! If you think cold, fizzy red wine is just too silly, we guess you could try a nice dry red with a little weight, to go with the heartier meat—Rhône, malbec, Corbières, aglianico, Rioja and zinfandel will all do.

Your spit-crankers deserve special attention. If it's cold out, keep them warm with hot apple cider laced with bourbon or rum. If it's summertime, give them a Mexican *chelada*—beer poured over ice in a glass with a salted rim, with lime juice squeezed in. These little treats will show you care, and keep your guests cranking!

THE MAGNIFICENT LAMB ROAST

- Whole Roast Lamb on a Spit
- Gürhan's Eggplant Salad
- Rice Pilaf with Cherries and Fennel
- Tamara's Mom's Cucumber Salad
- Dates with Almond Paste

Plan of Attack

1. Set up grill, start fire and begin to wrestle with lamb.

2. Grill vegetables for eggplant salad.

3. Put lamb on to roast.

4. Congratulatory toasts all around.

5. Make dates with almond paste.

6. Make cucumber salad.

7. Finish eggplant salad.

8. About an hour before lamb might be done, start rice.

9. Finish rice and let sit while carving up lamb.

10. Carnivore free-for-all!

11. When meat coma lifts, warm up dates.

How to Build the Lamb Grill

To follow our model, you'll need:

1 clean 50-gallon steel drum

Ten 8-by-8-inch cinder blocks

1 sheet flattened expanded metal (steel or stainless steel only), cut to 22 by 34 inches

1 wood dowel, 1⅛ inches in diameter and 6 feet long

1 wood dowel, ½ inch in diameter and 18 inches long

A drill, plus a ½-inch bit

Wood glue

We got our drum from a drum specialist (listed under "Drums" in the Yellow Pages, no less), but you may find one at a scrapyard, an army supply store or wherever survivalists congregate. We then had our friends cut it in half lengthwise in their metal shop. Not everyone has friends with these skills, however—so our suggestion is to *make* friends. Put a post on Craigslist in your area, for instance, that you'll need someone to cut a drum in half, and they get a bit of cash and an invitation to the party out of it. You might also look in the Yellow Pages for professional metalworkers in your area who may be able to help, or at least point you in the right direction. Trust us— people with metal saws are just itching to use them. While you're at it, you can screw a handle onto the second half of the drum, to better use it as a lid. Or, if you have expendable yard space, you could skip the barrel

A frame of cinder blocks supports the drum and the spit.

entirely and just dig a pit in the ground, then suspend the pole over it—Peter the Greek would approve, even if the dripping grease is not so great for the soil.

With our first setup, we were lucky enough to find a piece of I-beam that was just a little longer than the drum and wide enough to support it. It was monstrously heavy, however. For our second grill, we built a similar arrangement with cinder blocks. You'll want two more cinder blocks to stand up vertically at each end of the drum— they'll hold the spit at about the right height (a foot or so) above the flame. It's not shown in the illustration, but you can then lay the sheet of flattened, expanded metal

A simple handle for a wooden spit

(which is basically industrial-grade mesh) over the drum half, and you're good to grill meat and vegetables directly over the flame too.

For the spit itself, again we put our metalworking friends to work, and now we have a thin pole with an offset handle, plus a couple of prongs for holding the meat in place. If you go this route, just make sure you don't get anything galvanized, as our sculptor friends tell us that you don't want that stuff touching your food. But an easier option for your first lamb roast is to make a quickie spit out of wood dowels, cheaply acquired at your local lumber yard. Simply drill into the large dowel crosswise, an inch or two from one end. Then slip the smaller dowel into the hole, center it and secure with some wood glue—now you have something like a medieval steering wheel with which to crank the spit. It's not a permanent addition to your *batterie de cuisine,* but it will last for the whole lamb roast. And once you know how much fun this is, you can look into getting a steel spit of your own.

If you're feeling ambitious, you could chisel a shallow groove into the tops of the blocks, to keep the dowel in place. But even without that, your spit will stay relatively centered. Now get crankin'!

WHOLE ROAST LAMB ON A SPIT

Ingredients are pretty basic here, and your options for seasoning are wide open. The key elements are **a whole lamb** (duh), plenty of kitchen twine, **olive oil, garlic, salt** and **pepper.** And a *lot* of real wood charcoal, which burns hot and quick and gives the best flavor. (If you have to use the nasty little briquettes, at least avoid the chemical-soaked ones.) The brand we buy says, "This is the charcoal our ancestors used" on the label, and we like to contemplate that little primal connection while we crank the spit.

Where does one get a whole lamb, you ask? You'll want to track down a dedicated butcher, and you'll probably need to order the lamb a couple of weeks in advance. The bonus of going to a butcher is that the staff will likely get very excited about your project and give you all kinds of advice. If so, listen! That's how we learned. Where we live, some of the grocery stores have halal butchers who know all about the whole-lamb business. For that matter, there are also live-animal operations that slaughter lambs on demand—very handy, although the lamb's red meat does benefit a little from a couple of days' rest before cooking, which may be too much of a strain on your refrigerator facilities. Ask for one that's about 40 pounds dressed (closer to 60 pounds live weight)—we've done 75 pounds live weight and wound up with a staggering amount of meat, and anything less than 35 pounds can seem like not much yield for a whole lot of work, unless you happen to have someone attending the party who's very skilled with a carving knife. A 40-pounder will serve 20 with generous leftovers. If you live somewhere that lacks a good hands-on butcher, you may be able to arrange something over the Internet (see page 228); also see our suggestion for roasting a lamb in parts, page 206.

The butcher will (hopefully) chop the head and neck and the thinnest shank bones off. If you're a purist, you could keep the head on, but it will flop around and really become a liability in hour three. Also, removing it is a polite concession to guests who may be a little fearful about the whole lamb roast idea. Before you put the

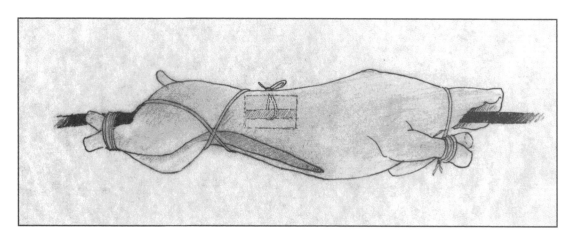

The bare minimum for stable trussing

carcass on the skewer, locate the tendon along the back of one of the rear shanks—make an incision underneath this, then slide the other shank through. Your lamb may look like it's primly crossing its legs, but in fact this tendon is one of the strongest pieces on the carcass, and it will hold throughout the roasting.

Next, you're ready to insert the spit. If you have a large-diameter spit, like the wood one we suggest, then slip it between the back legs, through the central cavity and out through the neck. If you have a smaller-diameter spit, you may be able to slip it through the back tendon, which is a bit more secure. Now start trussing the guy up. The goal is to minimize slippage around the spit—you don't want it spinning while the lamb just hangs there. Firmly tie the front legs together, then pull them as close to the spit as you can with twine; do the same with the back legs, adding a loop around the midsection. Finally, poke a hole along the spine and loop a piece of twine through, securing the spine to the spit. If in doubt, just tie more—or, as Karl says, "if you can't tie a knot, tie a lot."

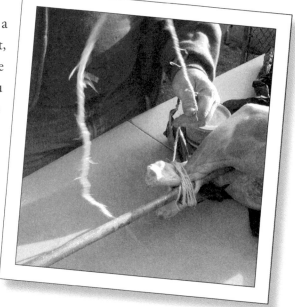

Karl ties up the lamb and makes it beg for mercy.

THE MAGNIFICENT LAMB ROAST

While the former Boy Scouts are busy trussing the lamb, someone else should be getting the fire going. Have the veggies for Gürhan's Eggplant Salad (page 207) ready to go on while the fire is high. When they're done, ideally the lamb will be all prepped.

But it probably won't. Because once you're done tying the thing up, then you need to slather the lamb with a very little bit of olive oil, salt and pepper. If you're really showing the lamb some love, you could stick little cloves of garlic under its skin, using a small, sharp knife to poke the holes. You could also make up about a quart mix of wine (red or white) and lemon juice, along with whatever spices you may like, to use as a basting liquid during the roasting process. Even Peter admits that this is kind of for show, but it looks impressive when it's swabbed on using a bunch of dill or fresh oregano as a brush.

So the lamb is finally ready to hoist over the fire. Just grab a couple of semiattentive guests and have them lift carefully from each end—it's a relatively straightforward process, compared with all that's come before. Actual flames should have died down, and the coals should have turned from black to red with a nice ash coating. Realistically, though, the fire will be plenty ready by the time you get the lamb secured on the spit—you can really just get the meat spinning, and tinker with the fire as you go. Keep the extra charcoal nearby; over the next few hours, you'll be tossing in more chunks every 20 or 30 minutes; lay them along the edges of the fire, rather than smack on top of the hot coals. We typically use about two 20-pound bags of wood charcoal per lamb roast. If you like, you can also toss in a couple of pieces of apple wood—or any other fragrant wood—for a little bit of smoke.

Now just crank, slowly but surely.

Repeat for approximately 4 hours. Bathroom breaks are allowed, but ideally, the meat should never stop moving. This is where you need to really turn on the charm, employing the old Tom Sawyer trick of making the task seem so fun and exciting that others will volunteer to do it for you. Bring beers or hot drinks, along with little snacks, to the people on spit-turning duty and tell them funny stories. The time will fly by.

At roughly hour 3, jab a meat thermometer in the leg. You're shooting for about 145°F, if you like your lamb rare; 155°F to 160°F for closer to medium. To reach this temperature will probably take about 4 hours, depending on how your fire's going and how big the lamb is. We prefer rarer meat and tend to err on that side, which has resulted in us putting the lamb out on the table only to realize that

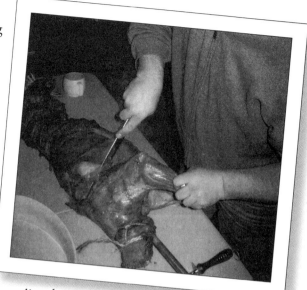

Karvin' Karl earns his nickname.

it's really *too* rare down close to the bone. In that case, we just slice off what's edible, and throw the rest in a big tray to finish off roasting in the oven at about 400°F. It ain't pretty, but it works just fine. Regardless, have the oven on so you can keep big hunks of lamb warm while you embark on cutting up the meat. Continue on with your powers of persuasion by handing knives and cutting boards to your (sober) guests and set to a group carving. It will make a daunting task far more manageable.

If you can keep the hungry hordes at bay, you can make up a nice platter full of meat slices and put that on the table, then go to work on more fiddly pieces, such as the ribs. But most likely, if you've done your job right, the carving table will simply be bum-rushed, and you'll wind up doling out hunks of meat right into waiting mouths. Just like our ancestors used to do.

The Not-So-Whole Roast Lamb

After our second lamb roast, we felt pretty good, but we didn't feel like we'd made absolutely the most delicious thing we could. Given the vagaries of the flame and our occasionally distracted approach to spit cranking, there was a fundamental problem that not all the meat on the animal was quite cooked to our liking. That's when our friend Ali stepped in. An Egyptian by birth and a New Yorker by force of personality, Ali was happy to tell us we were doing it all wrong.

"You have to cut it up!" he declared.

But, um, we were doing Whole. Roast. Lamb. What part didn't he understand?

"No, in pieces!" He proceeded to break it all down for us. Peter took furious notes. Ali scribbled instructions in Arabic, for us to hand-deliver to the Egyptian guy at the place where we usually bought our fresh-killed lamb. "But really, the Greeks—they're the best for this," he admitted.

We came away with a thorough plan and went straight to the nearest Greek butcher. We wound up with the most delicious lamb ever. It may not have been the amazing spectacle of a whole lamb—and it was a bit more work—but we felt like we'd made the most of the whole animal.

Ali's strategy involves breaking the

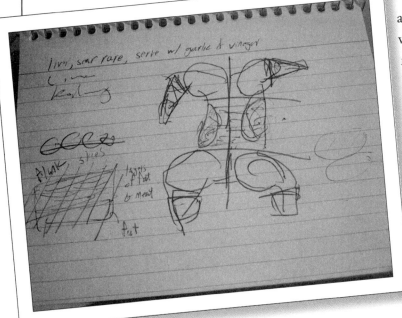

Peter's notes on Ali's lamb technique—amazingly, it worked

animal into major parts. You spit-roast just the legs and shoulders—not only are they easier to strap on the spit, but they cook more quickly as well. The ribs get sliced into chops, to be grilled directly over the flame near the end. The shanks you throw in the oven—braise them however you like, but we used saffron, preserved lemon and pomegranate molasses. The neck goes in a soup pot with celery, onion and carrot, to make a stock. The liver (if you request it from the butcher) gets seared in a pan with a splash of vinegar; brains get the same treatment. And the head gets cooked by tossing it on the coals after the initial roasting—a little dessert for the adventurous. (Or it can be . . . if you don't forget about it, only to discover it with horror the next morning, still in its plastic bag and sitting next to the computer. Er.)

GÜRHAN'S EGGPLANT SALAD

This is a wonderful little grilled-vegetable concoction that we had in Istanbul, cooked for us by a man named Gürhan on the rooftop of his apartment in the shadow of the Blue Mosque. The vinegar and garlic in the salad are a great flavor complement to the roasted lamb. Also, because you do the veg-roasting over a very high fire, it's a clever way to pass the time while you're waiting for the coals to burn down to the right temperature to roast the meat. You could also serve this as a bit of a Scooby snack before the meal itself—set it out with some warmed-up pita or nice crusty bread. *Serves 8*

3 medium eggplants

2 long semihot green chilies, such as Anaheim or Italian (see note)

2 ripe tomatoes

2 large red onions or 2 bunches scallions

6 or 7 cloves garlic

1 bunch fresh parsley

Olive oil

Red wine vinegar

1 lemon

Salt and pepper

Light the same grill that you intend to do the lamb on later. Wash the eggplants, chilies and tomatoes thoroughly and peel the onions. Place all the vegetables directly on the grill, as low over the fire as you can get them; no need for olive oil or other seasoning. Keep watch on your veggies, turning them when necessary to blacken them all over. Pull the chilies off first, as they should still have a little texture—you don't want them totally squishy. The eggplants and tomatoes can go longer—they should give nicely when you squeeze them with your tongs. All this can take anywhere from 8 to 15 minutes, depending on your fire and how big the vegetables are. Set all the finished vegetables in a bowl.

While they're cooling, peel your garlic and mince it very fine (or push it through a garlic press). Rinse your parsley and chop it fine.

When the veggies are cool enough to handle, cut off the stems and peel them carefully, but not obsessively—a few little bits of charred skin add flavor. Scrape the seeds out of the hot peppers.

Lay the eggplants out on a big cutting board and chop them up fine, almost into a pulp. (Gürhan had a wild double-knife technique, using both hands like some kind of Japanese steakhouse showman—impressive, but not necessary.) Scrape them into the bowl you'll be serving the salad in. Then do the same to the tomatoes, making sure to keep the juices. The onions and peppers also get chopped up, but not so furiously.

Add the garlic and most of the chopped parsley to the vegetables. Stir in enough olive oil to make the mixture a little silky—start with a glug, and go up from there. Add a splash of vinegar, then squeeze half the lemon over and taste—you want brightness, but not mouth-puckering tartness. Add more lemon if you like, then

That Amazingly Delicious Thing We Ate on Our Vacation, When We Were Pretty Drunk

Trying to re-create the magical flavors of some exotic trip is asking for trouble, but we try it all the time. After a quickie trip to Rome, we spent weeks obsessing over a particular sort of crustless white-bread sandwich we'd eaten every morning—it was made of oil-packed tuna, green tomatoes, basil and mayonnaise. We also had delicious cappuccinos topped with sweet coffee foam—only the language barrier kept us from figuring out how it was made. That's probably for the best, considering that the combination of the two would probably not taste quite as stellar in Queens.

Nonetheless, Tamara has begun many a Sunday Night Dinner invitation with the phrase "I just got back from . . . ," leading into a bonanza of Portuguese treats, or tasty things from Tennessee. But our 2005 trip to Istanbul was one of the most inspirational, because we got to help our new friend Gürhan cook in his own kitchen. Unlike in a restaurant, we were able to see just exactly what went into everything, including his "secret bachelor chicken." Even so, we haven't been able to re-create that dish perfectly, but at least whenever we make it and the eggplant salad Gürhan taught us, we think of our dreamy night at his apartment. Even if it's not perfect, it's still a great souvenir.

So next time you're traveling and eat something divine, make notes. Although you'll never be able to fully conjure the experience at home, often the flavor combinations will inspire you to cook something that is damn tasty in its own right.

season with salt and pepper. Let it sit at room temperature for at least 30 minutes, to let the flavors develop, and taste again before serving—you may need to adjust the salt and lemon again. Sprinkle the remaining parsley over the top and serve.

Notes:

- Check the peppers for heat before you get cooking. They should be relatively mild, but if you've gotten a spicier one, then scale back the amount you use. The peppers should lend only a subtle bite, not overwhelming heat.

- If you're preparing this salad on its own and don't care to light the grill, you can char the vegetables directly over your gas burner flame (a little messy) or under the broiler (be vigilant!).

RICE PILAF WITH CHERRIES AND FENNEL

This is one Turkish treat we didn't learn from Gürhan, but he did teach us an excellent technique, described here, for making the rice the perfect texture. The cherries turn the rice a pretty shade of pink, and the fennel lends a lovely softness to the whole thing. In lieu of dried cherries, you can use fresh—but make sure they are indeed sour. You can leave out the bulgur in a pinch, but it does give the pilaf a special toothsome quality. Garlic yogurt (page 72) is an excellent complement to this rice—so much so that Karl always stashes some away his for lunch the next day. *Serves 8*

1½ cups basmati or long-grain rice

½ cup dried sour cherries (see note)

1½ cups medium (#2) bulgur (see note)

1 large yellow onion

3 tablespoons butter

2 teaspoons fennel seeds

1 teaspoon granulated sugar

2 teaspoons salt

Set the rice to soak in a large bowl in plenty of cold water—leave it for 30 minutes. (If pressed for time, you can skip this step; however, it does rinse off the excess starch that may make your rice clump up.) Also soak the dried cherries in ½ cup hot water for 30 minutes. (This step is less skippable—it improves the cherries' texture and helps their flavor soak into the rice more easily.)

Set 2¼ cups water on to boil and measure the bulgur into another large bowl. While you're waiting, cut your onion lengthwise into thin slices. When the water has boiled, pour it over the bulgur, stirring to break up clumps. Cover and set aside, and occasionally fluff the grains with a fork—they will gradually absorb all the water.

In a large heavy saucepan with a tight-fitting lid, heat the butter on medium-high heat until bubbling. Throw in the fennel seeds and fry them for a few seconds, just until they begin to turn color and give off fragrance. Then add the onion, sugar and salt and sauté until the onion is limp and translucent. If it's turning brown, the pan is too hot and dry—reduce the heat and add a little extra butter. Drain the rice and add it to the saucepan with the onion. Stir gently and sauté until the rice begins to turn opaque—your aim is to get each grain nicely coated with butter. Drain the cherries and stir them, very gently, into the rice mixture. Pour in 2 cups water. Put the lid on and bring the rice to a boil, then turn down to a simmer.

After about 25 minutes, stick a fork down through the rice to check that all the water has been absorbed; once it has, remove the pan from the heat. Set it in an out-of-the-way spot; place a section of newspaper or a clean kitchen towel over the top of the pan, then replace the lid, pressing down to seal as well as you can. Over the next 20 or 30 minutes, the towel or paper will absorb the excess moisture and your rice will become perfectly fluffy. (This works even for Tamara, who used to be constitutionally unable to make rice.) Finally, stir the moistened bulgur into the rice. Mound on a platter or two and serve.

Notes:
- As on alternative to dried cherries, use 1¼ cups jarred Morello cherries, imported from Eastern Europe, and leave out the sugar.
- Bulgur is sold in three grinds, #1 being the finest and #3 the coarsest. The

THE MAGNIFICENT LAMB ROAST

fine grind would get lost in the rice, but #3 makes for an even chewier texture. If you use it, let it soak for a bit longer than the #2 grind.

TAMARA'S MOM'S CUCUMBER SALAD

Along with lamb and Gürhan's eggplant, the obvious accompaniment would be a Turkish-style cucumber-and-tomato salad. But we try not to get too theme-y in our menus. We like to mix traditions at least a little bit. This salad sports the same basic ingredients as a Turkish one, but the dressing draws on Tamara's German roots. It was a staple in her house as a kid, and it goes with a lot of different dishes we like to serve. Replacing the dill with fresh mint is a very fresh-tasting variation. *Serves 8*

4 large cucumbers or 8 small Persian cucumbers

1 large red onion

2 ripe tomatoes

Small bunch fresh dill

1 teaspoon granulated sugar

¼ cup cider vinegar

½ cup sour cream

1 lemon

Salt and pepper

Wash your cukes thoroughly. Peel them if you want, but Tamara uses what she calls the "texturing method" of dragging a fork down the length of the cuke to dig grooves into the skin. Slice the cucumbers very thinly and place them in a big glass or stainless-steel bowl. Cut the onion in half lengthwise and slice it into very thin half-rings. Add them to the bowl with the cukes. Chop the tomatoes coarsely and add them to the bowl, then chop the dill fine and add.

In a small bowl, whisk the sugar into the cider vinegar and taste. You want just enough sugar to take a little of the edge off the vinegar, but not enough to be sweet—adjust accordingly. Then whisk in the sour cream to form a smooth dressing. Finish with a squeeze of lemon, just to brighten it a bit, and salt and pepper to taste. Pour the dressing over the vegetables, toss and refrigerate for at least 30 minutes.

DATES WITH ALMOND PASTE

This dessert is a fittingly dainty end to a long night of feasting. The dates, stuffed with an earthy yet floral combination of ingredients, are rich but addictive, and people will probably eat as many as you give them, even to their detriment. Three apiece seems like a safe number—but you know your friends' appetites best. Because the dates can look a little paltry on a plate, we usually serve them with some seasonal fruit on the side: in warm weather, peaches or plums or berries, and in cold, apple slices with honey (Tamara likes chestnut honey, with a pinch of salt). *Serves 8*

24 good-quality large dates, preferably Medjool

7 ounces almond paste (see note)

1 tablespoon dark rum, plus more for garnish

1 tablespoon orange-flower water, plus more for garnish

Zest from 1 lemon

Preheat the oven to 400°F. Using a small knife or your fingers, pit the dates, trying to keep them relatively intact. With a fork, mash the almond paste with the rum, orange-flower water and zest. If the paste is too thick, add a teaspoon or two of water to loosen it a bit; the texture should be easily spreadable, but not runny.

Spoon this into the waiting dates. (You may have a bit of the filling left over.) Put the filled dates on a cookie sheet and bake for 10 minutes, until the dates get a little squishy and the almond paste is a little crunchy on top. Sprinkle with a few more drops of orange-flower water and rum and serve warm.

Notes:

- When shopping, be sure to is almond paste, rather than marzipan, which has a much larger amount of sugar. (Both are stocked in the baking aisle of most supermarkets.)
- As we suggest in the plan of attack, you can pit and fill the dates hours ahead and set them aside, covered. Then pop them in the oven just before serving.

Butter Up Your Purveyors

Big city, small town—no matter where you live, it behooves you to know the people you buy your food from. You don't have to be best friends with them (though it may end up that way), but a good relationship works wonders. Tamara greases the wheel by occasionally baking brownies for her butcher, produce guy and fishmonger. That's a bit extreme, but if you can spare the hour, the rewards will come back a thousand-fold. Plus, on a less selfish note, it is just old-fashioned nice, and you know in your heart there is plenty of room for *that* these days.

Ethics and fairness and customer-service bullshit aside, there is always secret "good stuff," either in the back or right under your nose, that the vendor knows about but you don't. And they love, love, *love* to share that with their favorite customers. A slightly fattier piece of meat can make the difference between dry and pure silk. A slightly brighter-eyed fish can make the difference between good and "Holy crap! Did you catch that today?" A crunchier cardoon can make your neighbor say, "I never even looked at these twice, but now I am making them tomorrow!" Plus, they're doing an unsung and important job for you: selecting the food that you will then take home and lovingly cook for family, friends and (hopefully) strangers—a remarkably intimate side to such a seemingly impersonal, capitalist transaction. Spread the love—your guests will feel it too.

FOR EXTRA CREDIT:
THE CROKE MONSTER

A towering cone of cream puffs stuck together with caramelized sugar, a croquembouche ("crunch in the mouth") is traditionally served as a French wedding cake. The happy couple cracks into the hardened-sugar glaze with a sword, and guests tear off the cream puffs with their hands. That's the kind of ceremony we like!

We have made one for a wedding, but in general we've busted out the Croke Monster, as we've come to call our rather, shall we say, "rustic" version, as an additional over-the-top element at an already over-the-top dinner. Case in point: The first time we made the Croke (we're now on familiar enough terms that we can call it that) was for the same New Year's party where we were roasting the whole pig and the whole lamb. Crazy much? This Frenchie work of dessert architecture is literally the pinnacle of our achievements.

So if you like a challenge, follow our lead. The results are divine, but the process of making it can be slightly satanic. If you lose stamina in the middle, remember that the rare baker who makes the thing will charge at least $3 *per cream puff*, so you're saving a fantastic amount of money. And the feeling of accomplishment when you place the last cream puff on top is incomparable—all-powerful you will have transformed flour, sugar, butter and eggs into an amazing dessert that's both delicious and structurally sound.

The funny thing about this dessert is that it is not hard at all (except for the math—we'll get to that later). The cream puffs are made from an easy pastry called pâte à choux, cooked on the stove top and relatively indestructible. The filling is a fairly straightforward custardlike pastry cream—and you could make it even easier by using sweetened whipped cream instead.

But then you get to the part involving the hot caramel. This seemingly innocuous combo of sugar and water has the power to burn your skin right off, as it sticks and continues burning, even as you try desperately to wash it away. Scared yet? Maybe if we make it seem dreadful, you'll be extra careful—and pleasantly surprised at how few scars you end up with. Our per-Croke burn count is finally down to a very boring zero.

If you're now holding the book at arm's length and thinking this will be the point where you tell your friends, "Yeah, I cooked through that book, but that Croke thing . . . that looked like some scary shit, so I left it alone"—*don't*. Stay and Make. The. Croke. You will feel so empowered (and have such an excellent sugar high) that you'll be glad you did. Who knows? You may even be as crazy as we are and do it multiple times!

Do the Math

The first time Tamara made a croquembouche, she thought, "I know this recipe says to make the bottom ring out of thirteen puffs, but I want mine to be a little bigger. Say, sixteen puffs?" Thanks to the wonders of geometry, that seemingly minor enlargement really meant she needed an extra fifty-one puffs to complete her tower—nearly fifty percent more. She didn't discover this until halfway through the construction, so she had to go back and make more puffs in the middle of the operation. There are few things in life as sad as a half-finished croquembouche—it looks like a ruined coliseum. Worse, it was 6 P.M., and guests were due to arrive at 6:30 P.M.—there was not enough booze in the world to quell the panic.

Recalling this horror, we now always sit down and think very seriously about the scale of our Croke—we make little drawings, bust out the π formulas and add up a lot of numbers. But then we also always end up getting impatient and just starting to build. What we pretty consistently do now is a modest sixty puffs, with twelve puffs around the base. (By contrast, Tamara's fateful base-16 structure wound up requiring 168 puffs.) It's 8 inches across the bottom and stands about a foot tall. If you're thinking that's not very big, remember that even your most sugar-crazed guests can handle only about four cream puffs each.

Do of course feel free to make your own Croke larger—just remember that even a small increase in the base diameter will call for a significant number more puffs. (Believe us, we've tried to work out a formula for this, but our math skills are rusty, and the puffs are too irregularly shaped.) And we also encourage you to freestyle—pile up your cream puffs in the shape of a rugged mountain range, for instance. But in this case, you ought to do some kind of rough sketch, to make sure it will be structurally sound, and to get a clear idea how many puffs you need to complete your vision.

THE CROKE MONSTER

This recipe makes enough for about sixty 2-inch puffs, just enough to assemble a 1-foot-tall tower. If you're feeling nervous, you can always make another half-batch of puffs as insurance against breakage and your assistants sneaking bites on the sly—and you'll have enough pastry cream to fill most of the extras. Some people will try to sell you a cone-shaped mold to construct your Croke around. Bullshit. We've never used one, and we've been fine. If your cream puffs are thoroughly coated in caramel and held in place until the sugar hardens and bonds it to its neighbors, you will have a remarkably stable structure.

And like we said, not much of this is too tricky—but the pâte à choux for the pastry puffs calls for a little upper-body strength. Tamara likes to power through and do it all in one go; Zora divides the recipe in half, doing one half-batch, then whipping up the second half while the first puffs are baking. *Serves 15 or so*

For the filling:

2 cups milk

¾ cup granulated sugar

6 large egg yolks

4 tablespoons cornstarch

1 tablespoon vanilla extract

1½ teaspoons almond extract and/or 1 tablespoon
   orange-flower water

1¼ cups (2½ sticks) butter, softened

For the pastry puffs:

2 cups water

1 cup (2 sticks) butter

½ teaspoon salt

2½ cups all-purpose flour

10 large eggs

For the caramel:

4 cups granulated sugar

1 cup water

2 teaspoons lemon juice or apple cider vinegar

Make the filling: In a heavy saucepan, set 1 cup milk and the sugar over high heat. While you're waiting for the milk to boil, whisk the remaining 1 cup milk, egg yolks and cornstarch together in a large bowl. As soon as the milk boils, turn the heat down to low, then *slowly* pour about a third of the hot milk into the egg-yolk mixture, stirring constantly with a wooden spoon or whisk, then return that gradually to the milk in the pan, continuing to stir like a fiend. Turn the heat back up to medium and keep stirring until the whole business thickens, which takes only 2 or 3 minutes. Never let the liquid get up to a full boil—otherwise you'll end up with very sweet scrambled eggs, and there is no saving that. Take the pan off the heat, stir in the vanilla, almond extract and/or orange-flower water and transfer everything to a bowl; cover with plastic wrap and refrigerate until thoroughly chilled, at least 3 hours.

There's one more step to finish this, but you should get the puffs going at this stage. First, though, be sure you've taken the butter for the filling out of the fridge to soften up.

Make the puffs: Preheat the oven to 425°F. Combine the water, butter and salt in a large, heavy saucepan set over high heat. As soon as the water comes to a boil, remove the pan from the heat and dump in the flour all in one go. Stir vigorously with a wooden spoon until the mixture forms a thick dough and pulls away from the sides of the pan.

Return the pan to the heat and cook, stirring constantly, for 2 minutes or so. When the dough is glossy and leaves a thin film on the bottom of the pan, take the pan off the heat again. Let the dough cool briefly, then vigorously start beating in the eggs, one at a time, making sure each egg is completely incorporated. Unless you're an Olympic rower, your arms will get tired. Keep at it—the point when it comes together, in a thick, shiny, smooth mass, is really satisfying.

Get out a baking sheet. Using two spoons, scoop walnut-size drops of dough (about 1½ tablespoons) onto the baking sheet, about 1 inch apart. This produces puffs that are a generous 2 inches in diameter; if you want a daintier Croke, you can scale down the size of the puffs to 1 tablespoon each, but any smaller and they'll be difficult to fill. Bake 10 minutes, then reduce the heat to 350°F and continue to bake until well browned, another 10 minutes or so. Immediately remove the puffs from the pan to a rack (if they stick, let them sit for a minute and try again). When they're cool enough to handle, take a chopstick and poke a hole in one side, to let the steam out. This will also be the hole where you pipe in the filling.

Finish the filling and stuff the puffs: When you're ready to move on, put the butter for the filling in a large bowl and beat it with a mixer until it's pale and fluffy. Pour in the cold filling and beat until smooth, 3–4 minutes. Cover and refrigerate the whole concoction until you're ready to fill the puffs.

Spoon the filling into a pastry bag fitted with a plain ¼-inch tip.

Oh, as if. You probably don't have a pastry bag, and Karl's the only person we know who's picky enough to use one. So spoon the filling into a quart-size ziplock bag (freezer-weight plastic is easiest to manage), squeeze out the air and seal it up. Then cut a tiny hole in the corner, and stick that corner just inside the puff and squeeze in the filling—but with restraint. If you fill the puffs to capacity, they're too heavy to dip in the caramel easily. This step is more fun when attacked by two people.

FOR EXTRA CREDIT

Once you've filled all your puffs, you should take stock and check your math again, and make sure you have enough of them to build your Croke. Congratulate yourself with a drink—a nice dessert wine goes very nicely with what comes next.

Make the caramel and build the fucker: Divide the sugar, water and lemon juice between two saucepans—ideally steel or light enamel, so you can see the caramel darken. Stir to dissolve, then cover and bring to a boil. Boil for about 2 minutes with the lids on, to steam any sugar crystals off the sides of the pans, then remove the lids and continue to boil until the sugar turns dark amber, 15–20 minutes.

While this is going on, set up your construction site: Get out a big serving platter or tray to build the Croke on; measure an 8-inch-diameter circle, so you know what you're shooting for. Lay out a wet towel, as well as some tiny tongs or a couple of the smallest forks you have (our tool of choice happens to be oyster forks stolen—but not by us!—from a nice casino restaurant). You should be ready to roll before the sugar syrup has started to color, so you can keep an eye on it as it starts to darken.

When the caramel hits the color of a good bock or amber beer, remove both pans from the heat. You'll work with one pan of caramel, and when it starts getting too thick, you'll reheat the second pan gently. Remember: Caramel is dangerous—so from here on out, treat it as your beautiful enemy. If you do get some of the hot sugar on your skin, pat it immediately with your wet towel to stop the burn. Carefully dip a cream puff into the caramel, covering at least the bottom half of it. Place it on the tray. Repeat, choosing your largest puffs first, to form a circle of about 12 puffs, depending on how big your puffs wound up being. Make the next level of puffs the same size, then start reducing the number to form a conical tower. Think of yourself as a dessert mason—the caramel is your mortar, and you have to let it set. Of course, while you're letting it harden on the growing Croke tower, it's also hardening up in the cooling pan. Again, it helps to have two people, so one can reheat the caramel as necessary, or even whip up a fresh batch.

After you place the final puff, stand back and admire your artistry. Tremble at your power! This is your Ayn Rand moment.

If you're not so Bauhaus and want to make the thing pretty, you can drizzle the remaining caramel around with a spoon, pulling it into thin filaments of sugar, so it sits in a haze of spun sugar. We've only ever done this by accident—the caramel has to be just the right thickness. If you manage to pull it off, send us a picture.

For authenticity, crack the thing open with a sword, wielded by the most sober person in the room.

Caramel Cleanup

You did the math, you built the Croke, you beat the caramel . . . and while you were doing a victory lap around the kitchen, the sugar hardened into a rock on the bottom of your pan. Don't curse us as the two bitches who ruined your good cookware. Just fill the pan with water and boil until the sugar all melts off, usually about 10 minutes. Voilà—another pan saved.

Last Words

This may be the end of the book, but we hope it's only the beginning of your cooking adventure. We hope the friends you feed will in turn start cooking for their friends, and they'll cook for their friends, and so on. Maybe the whole circle will come around, and one day you'll be inviting us to dinner.

In the meantime, visit us at our website, **forkingfantastic.com,** and tell us how it goes. You can browse through photos and videos from our Sunday Night Dinners—and you can post some of your own endeavors. You'll also find more general cooking tips, as well as more information on wine—specific vineyards and labels to look out for, all for cheap. And we have a whole page devoted to excellent kitchen music—from Mahalia Jackson to the Ramones to "Azz & Tittiez."

The great thing about cooking is that there's always room to be better, always something new to learn. Even if you were crazy enough to make every single recipe in this book, you can't rest on your laurels. The world of food and flavor is infinite, and your friends will probably be asking for something new soon. If you're anything like us, one flavor will lead you to another book that combines it with something else, and on to another, and soon enough you'll be cooking food from halfway around the world.

So keep exploring and experimenting—we do. In our **Further Reading** section that follows, we suggest a few of our favorite inspirational cookbooks and other sources. And if you're having trouble finding ingredients in your area or need some guidance with cookware, flip to the **Where to Get the Goods** page.

Thanks for reading. Keep the heat up and the wine flowing, and cook something fucking fantastic for us!

In love and garlic,
Tamara and Zora

Good work, hungry kiddies!

FURTHER READING

TAMARA RECOMMENDS:

James Beard's American Cookery, by James Beard. Old Americana, staples and flavor combinations that are largely forgotten but should not be. Dishes like tipsy parson, tongue-and-spinach salad and blueberry grunt are represented beautifully. Written in a clear voice by a good cook who truly loved what he did.

Mastering the Art of French Cooking, by Julia Child, Louisette Bertholle and Simone Beck. The. Bible.

Sunday Suppers at Lucques, by Suzanne Goin with Teri Gelber. A serious go-to at the Reynolds/Wasserman Love Shack. Great ideas that simply let the excellent ingredients speak for themselves; recipes are organized seasonally, and flavor combinations are interesting and completely accessible. Two words: Gentlemen's Relish.

The Whole Beast, by Fergus Henderson. Genius who teaches creative frugality through humor. Trained as an architect before becoming a chef, he opened St. John in London in 1995 and immediately became the chef all chefs wanted to visit. He makes offal sound like more fun than a barrel of monkeys. The follow-up, *Beyond Nose to Tail,* with Justin Piers Gellatly, includes Karl's favorite, Dr. Henderson's Ice Cream.

The Taste of Country Cooking, by Edna Lewis. An incredibly beautiful book-length essay on growing up in a town founded by freed slaves. Miss Lewis's love of the land and the bounty that it gave her community is breathtaking. The recipes all have stories of special holidays, dinners, lunches and breakfasts, with and for friends and family, all guided by the seasons and what was available. The introduction alone still makes me tear up, and I can be a tough bitch. Edna remains one of the most powerful voices that speaks to my cooking. I also like her *In Pursuit of Flavor,* which presents food based on where it comes from:

barnyard, fields, and so on. *The Gift of Southern Cooking*, written with Scott Peacock, is well done, but feels modernized in comparison with her earlier books.

Larousse Gastronomique, by Prosper Montagne. An amazing encyclopedia of French food. There are no measurements—just loose instruction. That was freeing for me, but may be freakout-inducing for others. The updated 2001 edition is relatively modernized, though still fascinating; I have my grandfather's 1961 edition, with a particularly inspiring black-and-white photo of a baked Alaska.

Au Pied de Cochon, by Martin Picard. One of the most fabulous books ever, and self-published in its first edition to boot! Au Pied de Cochon is a restaurant in Montreal where they cook using the whole animal and then throw in foie gras. For fun. And so much of it that I actually couldn't finish my whole serving—it was like *Sophie's Choice.* Amazing food and brilliant design—and the first edition is well worth the price.

Spice, by Ana Sortun. Ingenious book organized by spice flavor combinations. Her ideas are fresh yet rooted in authentic Middle Eastern and Mediterranean traditions. Very powerful—makes us both want to run to the store and turn on the oven.

ZORA RECOMMENDS:

The Joy of Cooking, by Irma Rombauer and Marion Rombauer Becker. It's not flashy, but it's a fantastic reference, whether you need to know how much all-purpose flour to substitute for cake flour or how to skin a squirrel (step on its tail, then yank). It also has great standard recipes for baked goods. Look for older, secondhand editions, to get all the squirrel-skinning details. The 1997 revamp is good too, as it has more appealing meat and vegetable recipes, but don't get the 75th-anniversary edition—too kitschy.

The Supper of the Lamb, by Robert Farrar Capon. Like the *Moby-Dick* of cookbooks—full of beautiful biblical language, surprisingly hilarious commentary and tons of obscure information, it pretends to be a cookbook but winds up as a manifesto. The chapter on onions made me cry on the subway, and I'm not even into the God stuff.

The Omnivore's Dilemma, by Michael Pollan. Just plain smart. Pollan is a brilliant writer who puts his personal eating experience in the context of the larger American food machine. If that's too weighty for you, pick up *In Defense of Food,* which is basically the CliffsNotes version. And his 2002 book *Botany of Desire* is not so explicitly political, but just as insightful.

Madhur Jaffrey Indian Cooking, by Madhur Jaffrey. If you're curious about Indian food, start here. Jaffrey is clear and concise and makes everything seem manageable. This book, along with a subscription to *Cook's Illustrated,* is basically how I learned to cook. Get it just for the Lake Palace Eggplant recipe.

The Naked Chef Takes Off, by Jamie Oliver. The first cookbook I read that encouraged not measuring—a huge breakthrough. This book also encouraged me to make fresh pasta (so worth it!) and demystified risotto. The sweet stuff suffers from the imprecision, but every savory dish I've ever made from this book has been delicious—and never sinks under unnecessary restaurant-y complication.

Cook's Illustrated. Yes, it's the world's most boring magazine, entirely in black-and-white. Yes, Christopher Kimball is perhaps the most righteous, annoying twit in the food universe. And you should never, ever read his editor's letter, or you'll throw up. But as a way to learn *why* food does what it does when you cook it, *Cook's Illustrated* is invaluable—at least for me. (Tamara, on the other hand: "I can't hack that shit. Just read it to me if I must know it.") Get a year's subscription for manageable bimonthly doses of I-did-not-know-that, then maybe sign up for the online database, a trove of perfected standard recipes.

WHERE TO GET THE GOODS

We know we're at a huge food advantage living in New York City, where we can buy any ingredient except maybe whale blubber. But we didn't realize how difficult life can be out in less diverse quarters until a friend of Zora's reported she couldn't find small red chilies, the kind she was in the habit of crushing up into flakes, as needed, for many of her Italian recipes—and this was in Boston! Zora sent her an emergency care package, along with a tip from Peter: "Next time, try Chinatown." Indeed, Chinese, Korean, Indian and Mexican groceries usually have not only a great selection of small dried red peppers, but also fresh herbs that put those at the supermarket to shame, both in attractiveness and price.

With creative cross-ethnicity shopping, we rarely have to leave our neighborhood for specialty items. We buy "Japanese" eggplants at Indian stores and often use Mexican *crema* instead of harder-to-find French crème fraîche. It pays to think beyond the standard land borders when you do your food shopping.

But if you've exhausted your neighborhood resources, we recommend the following people for hard-to-find meats, spices and cookware, as well as Victoria's magical folding table with chairs.

MEATS AND POULTRY

D'ARTAGNAN

dartagnan.com

The duck experts—French, *mais oui,* but based in New Jersey. Order whole birds and fat, as well as sausages, truffles and the like.

HERITAGE FOODS USA

heritagefoodsusa.com

Save rare-breed farm animals by eating them! You must taste a Red Wattle pig at least once in your life; you can also order an excellent Thanksgiving turkey, plus bison, lamb, duck and more, all humanely raised on small farms.

Shepherd's Lamb
organiclamb.com

Certified organic, grass-fed lamb produced on a family farm in the mountains of New Mexico. These are some tasty little sweethearts.

Niman Ranch
nimanranch.com

The biggest online source for humanely raised, antibiotic-free meat, including ground meat, roasts, odd bones and variety meats (no whole lamb, though).

SPICES

Kalustyan's
kalustyans.com

A New York City institution with a boggling stock of spices, beans, grains, dried fruits and nuts, even preserved lemons. The website catalog can be overwhelming, but stick with it—you'll find pomegranate molasses, sumac and Aleppo pepper, among other tasty things.

Penzeys Spices
penzeys.com

For everything from various blends of curry to double-strength vanilla, all at very reasonable prices. We recommend it as an alternative to Kalustyan's primarily because its website is less crazy-making, and it's great for more common herbs and spices too.

COOKWARE

Le Creuset
lecreuset.com

The definitive makers of enameled cast-iron cookware, with beautiful Dutch ovens that will last through the ages. The sort of thing you register for as a wedding gift. No online ordering here—but department stores often have midwinter sales on the stuff.

LODGE CAST IRON

lodgemfg.com

Cast-iron skillets, preseasoned or not, as well as good-quality enameled pots and Dutch ovens, in the style of Le Creuset but a lot cheaper.

THE MAGICAL FOLDING TABLE

THE FURNITURE DOMAIN

thefurnituredomain.com

The source for Victoria's fabulous wood folding table that fits four chairs inside, for maximum efficiency—search for "Space Saver Dining Set."

PEOPLE WE LOOOVE

ZORA O'NEILL

I'm grateful first to my parents, Beverly McFarland and Patrick O'Neill, for raising me to appreciate food—and for making me eat salad every night. I also learned a lot from the late, great Barton Rouse, of Terrace Flaming Club. From the butcher-paper menus and "*les vins*" to White Trash Cooking and pigs on spits, Barton's flair is a model I follow every day, along with his simple equation, food = love. Speaking of love, thanks to Peter Moskos, for being there since 1992, even though you didn't realize it; your patience is sublime. And to Karine Schaefer: Here's to theme cakes and quality control.

Back in grad school, I had a big kitchen and a great crew of housemates—thanks to James Conlon, Jennifer Rawlings-Clark and Jeremy Rich for being willing to eat anything. Sorry we never got that baby goat. . . . Likewise, thanks to Aaron Seeskin, another long-suffering roommate, who put up with a lot more bacon fat than he had to. Right after September 11, 2001, I ran a supper club called Operation Roving Gastronome. Boring old financial necessity forced me to shelve it, but I am grateful to all the guests and hosts of ORG, especially Tal Rachleff and Livia Alexander, who were so supportive and kept me on the cooking track. The spirit of those parties lives on in Sunday Night Dinner—I'm glad to see that the popularity of dining at home wasn't just a temporary reaction to terrorism.

This cookbook could not have happened without all the Sunday Night Dinner regulars—among them, Katie Trainor, who brought the Wednesday Night Dinner love from Boston; Christopher Calderhead, who ate and illustrated; Dapper Dan, who appears to be the axis around which the universe revolves; and our friend and agent, Gillian MacKenzie, who probably didn't know what a long-term project she was getting into when she first came to dinner. But we're so glad she did.

Special thanks to the old-schoolers who gave feedback while we were developing recipes, and to the fine crew of testers who helped iron out the kinks (er, sorry about that ham!): Cristina Topham, Josh Hebert, Larra Nebel, Sara Straus and Kristina Carroll. Anna Utevsky offered bacon brainstorming, Heather Hughes test-drove the Croke, and Neil Doshi inspired a date breakthrough. For the cassoulet, Catherine Harris and Andres Rodriguez consulted from afar, and I also got excellent advice from the eGullet community.

I also doubt this cookbook would've happened anywhere but Astoria, my home sweet home in New York City. There's a whole world of taste just in this patch of Queens, and I'm honored to be a citizen. For more than a decade, it has been my pleasure to explore—even in the teeming aisles of Trade Fair. Thanks to every shop owner who has ever sold me some ingredient and told me how to cook it. And that includes Ali El Sayed, whose Kabab Café has been a second home— *merci, habibi.*

And final thanks to Karl, for being the ultimate roadie (who also happens to take photos and do pastry), and Tamara, for getting the show on the road. And to our editor, Lucia Watson, who got the project from the instant she read the original title. Hell, yes!

TAMARA REYNOLDS

I would like to thank: my husband, Karl, without whom not one meal would be possible; he has truly been the man behind the curtain, and thank Christ he loves me "because of" and not "in spite of." My good friends far and near for always being game to come over and try some crazy-ass idea that made its way into my oven, and every friend and stranger who has ever gotten on the N train to come to Astoria for dinner. Ali, for generously sharing the world of Steinway Street and all things Egyptian, political, and beyond. Grant, for telling me when I was worthy of the real South; Victoria, for years and years of all beautiful things Italian; Mary Ann, for close counsel and reminders that not everyone cares what kind of butter it is; Golden, for the dancing, the love and that floating $200. Peter, for always being game to cook in the middle of the night. Christopher, for jumping in as surrogate host when I was freaking out in the kitchen, and for marrying Karl to me. Karine, for the Vermont "retreats," the excellent perspective and the friendship. Gillian, for being a great agent, but also a friend, and believing I could write long before I did. Clamshack, for being the first to dream *Booktour! The Musical* with me. Amanda, for coming to dinner and opening Penguin's door to us, and Lucia, for being such a great eater, editor and believer.

My parents, Paul and Tonya, for giving me a home of good food even though I was too ridiculous to appreciate it; Dona and Ron, for the years of unconditional love and support; Victor and Dottie, for taking me in and loving me like their own; and Steve, Jill and Joan for always being very loving and hungry cheerleaders.

I would also like to thank Brad for his patience and encouragement when I decided to learn to cook, and *Gourmet* magazine for being my tutor. (It was a very long learning curve, people.) And thanks to every cook who has ever generously given me ideas and guidance: Lynn McNeely, Ashley Archer, Millicent Souris, Colin Alevras, Liza Queen, Gabrielle Hamilton, Michael Recchiuti, Matt Hamilton, Melissa Fernandez and Ian Knauer. Heather (Mr. Shit), for introducing me to Edna Lewis. Every cook who has written a book that has made me pore over it well into the night, picking up ideas and inspiration. All of the unsung grandmothers who have passed on family recipes for generations. My butchers, Big John and Little John, and all of the guys at International Meat Market, who were as generous with their meat as they were with advice and ideas. The butchers at Acropolis for always having excellent aged meat, a kiss and a drink. Patrick, Sarah and all of the fabulous people at Heritage Foods USA for their generosity with the "apartment pickup special," and their dedication to keeping some of the best eating breeds alive. All of the staff at Elliniki Agora in Astoria, the best neighborhood produce market a budding cook could hope for. Nikos and Eleni from Greek House in Astoria for always having that hard-to-find item, the best stuffed grape leaves and plenty of encouragement. The boys at Dave and Tony's Salumeria for running such an old-school kick-ass Italian store (against the odds!) in the neighborhood. All of the guys at the old Fulton Fish Market and the new Hunts Point Fish Market, but especially Blue Ribbon Fish for being so helpful and doing such honest and excellent work while the rest of us slackers are sleeping. The Trade Fair on 30th Avenue for all of the inspiration they have provided by simply acknowledging when someone new moves into the hood. Late to the game but no less important is Vishnu, my fish man, for going above and beyond to get what I needed.

Thank you to every corner of our Sunday Night Dinner community for showing up. It is always such a pleasure to see your hungry faces.

Thanks to Led Zeppelin, the Rolling Stones and all of those other unbelievably talented and long-dead roots and gospel singers who kept me company late nights when I was alone in the kitchen.

Zora, without whom this great adventure would have taken a very different shape, if at all.

And finally Dapper Dan, for being the Great Connector and generously sharing everything he has ever had. Without him, I am not sure any of this would be possible. He is a once in a lifetime.

INDEX

Note: Entries in **bold** refer to dinner party menus; page numbers in *italics* refer to illustrations (those followed by *c* refer to the color insert photos); page numbers followed by a *t* refer to information found in text boxes.